The Dictionary Of
STRUM & PICKING PATTERNS

By Fred Sokolow

To access audio visit:
www.halleonard.com/mylibrary

1325-0252-6137-5111

SPECIAL THANKS TO RONNY SCHIFF
FOR HER ASSISTANCE WITH THIS BOOK

HAL•LEONARD®
CORPORATION

7777 W. BLUEMOUND RD. P.O. BOX 13819 MILWAUKEE, WI 53213

TABLE OF CONTENTS

INTRODUCTION

Whether you play alone or with others, professionally or just for fun, chances are that much of your playing will not be just hot licks and fiery solos; it will be accompaniment. Your guitar backs up your voice, someone else's, or another soloing instrument. *But what kind of accompaniment will you play?*

There are so many kinds of guitar backup: a hard-driving, rock-boogie lick; a lazy, fingerpicking blues pattern; a honky-tonk country strum; a syncopated scratch-rhythm to a funk groove; a relaxed calypso strum; a grungy, punkish thrash; and a gentle, fingerpicked folk ballad arpeggio to name a few. Playing the right backup with a good groove is as much an art form as soloing.

This book has a strumming or picking pattern for nearly any rhythmic groove you are likely to hear in rock, blues, soul/funk, metal, folk, punk, or country music. The patterns are grouped in these musical categories to make it easy for you to find the feel you want.

Of course, many songs cannot be neatly pigeonholed in one category, and all musical styles cross-breed. A country tune in the nineties may have a seventies rock groove, and a heavy-metal back-up guitar part may come straight from a twenties Delta blues strum. At the end of each chapter, there are cross-referencing notes to help you find the rock strum that is hiding in your favorite country tune (or the country-picking pattern hiding in your favorite rock tune!).

Most strums are written with rhythm slashes: ♩ ♪ ♫ ♫ ♩. These slashes have standard rhythmic notation: There are ties, rests, eighth notes, quarter notes, etc. Fingerpicking patterns are written in tablature and standard music notation. The best news of all is that *every strum or picking pattern is played on the matching recording that comes with the book.* Each pattern is repeated a few times to establish the groove. So learn each strum by reading, listening, and playing along with the recording. Occasionally, an *equipment note* will suggest the type of guitar (electric or acoustic) or electronic effect (echo, distortion, chorus) best suited to the pattern.

Strumming

Most people strum with a flatpick, some just use their fingers. If you prefer using your fingers, strum *down* with the fingernails of several fingers at once (or just the index finger) and *up* with the thumb. Either way, strumming can consist only of downstrokes or of a combination of up and down-strokes.

If a strumming pattern has down and upstrokes, there are two general rules: The first is strum *down* on the *downbeats, up* on the *upbeats* or *"and" beats*. For example, in a strum made of eighth notes:

In a strum made of sixteenth notes, this pattern is doubled up and upstrokes are between the downbeats and the "and" beats:

The second rule is **keep your wrist going *down-up-down-up* smoothly, even when there are rests or tied notes.** During the spaces that rests or tied notes indicate, keep the rhythmic *down-up* wrist action going, but don't strike the strings. This makes your rhythm flowing and musical.

Play the following two examples; don't strike the strings when the arrows are in parenthesis.

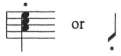

Damping

Sometimes you play staccato chords (clipped, with no sustain) by muting or damping the strings after strumming them. There are two ways to stop the strings from vibrating: touch them with the palm of your picking hand, or (if you are fretting the strings) release the fretting pressure so that your fingers are touching the strings but not pressing them down to the fretboard. Either way, a damped note has a dot over it:

If a chord is damped by your fretting hand *before* you strum it, it is written like this:

Fingerpicking

Most popular styles of fingerpicking (blues, rock, country) make use of the thumb and one or two fingers. The thumb usually picks the lower three (bass) strings; the index and middle fingers play the top three (treble) strings. Occasionally, the ring and little fingers also pick treble strings.

Players who do a lot of fingerpicking often wear a thumbpick (plastic or metal) and a finger-pick or two (on the index and perhaps the middle finger). If you play a steel-string guitar, the picks make you sound louder and clearer and save wear and tear on your fingers.

The fingerpicking patterns are written in tablature and standard notation. In standard notation:

• Notes that are plucked by the thumb have stems pointing *down.* (♩)

• Notes picked by the fingers have stems pointing *up.* (♩)

Practicing

Here's a step-by-step method for learning a strumming or picking pattern:

1. Read about the pattern. If you know any of the tunes mentioned in the notes, think about their rhythm groove.

2. Listen to the pattern on the recording. Track numbers are indicated by the following symbol: ◆

3. Play the pattern over and over. Most are one bar long; some are two bars. Play it several times and get the groove to match the recording.

4. Play a tune that has that rhythmic feel and use the pattern as your accompaniment. If you have a recording of a tune with the same feel, try playing along with it.

5. Find other tunes with that same groove in songbooks, especially ones that are familiar to you, and use the pattern as accompaniment. Once you can do this, the pattern is yours and it's part of your repertory.

A few practical tips:

- Each rhythm pattern has a name that is used to identify it in the book and on the recording.

- There is a tempo indication under the name, to the left.

- Rhythm slash patterns include a boxed chord grid located to the right of the tempo indication. It shows the chord that is played on the recording.

BLUES: THE ROOTS OF ROCK

The blues is an African-American music form derived from spirituals and work songs, but it has evolved and developed in tandem with European musical forms and has affected all American music. This chapter covers picking and strumming styles of rural "folk" blues, which goes back as far as the beginning of the twentieth century, and urban electric blues styles of the 1940s up to the present.

The strums and picking patterns of both urban and rural blues are used in rock, country, folk, heavy metal, and funk/soul music. For example, the Travis-picking of country and rockabilly grew out of blues fingerpicking, and the boogie-woogie guitar backup style of rock and heavy metal goes directly back to rural blues guitar backup.

Since so many guitar styles grew out of the blues, this chapter is a good starting place for a study of guitar backup. As you listen to and play the patterns, don't assume that "rural" strums can only be played on acoustic guitar and "urban" patterns must be electric. There has always been crossover, so try all the blues strums and picking patterns acoustically and electrically.

Contemporary electric blues guitarists often set their tunes to a rock or funk beat, in addition to using the traditional blues shuffle. Check the **ROCK** and **R&B/FUNK/SOUL** chapters for the appropriate backup patterns.

Rural Blues Shuffle, Strum #1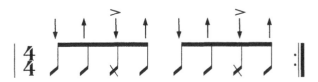

Tempo: Moderate to fast shuffle

Through the 1950s and even into the 1960s, most blues guitarists (especially acoustic players) used their thumb and fingers. In this strum, you brush down with your thumb and up with your fingers. Damp the strings with the palm of your picking hand. Use for moderate tempos like "Help Me" (Sonny Boy Williamson) and "Pride and Joy" (Stevie Ray Vaughan), or faster tunes like "Baby Please Don't Go" (Lightnin' Hopkins, Van Morrison, and many others have recorded it).

Rural Blues Shuffle, Strum #2

Tempo: Fast shuffle

This is for faster shuffles in the "Boogie Chillun" (John Lee Hooker) vein. For a percussive effect and to enhance the beat, slap the strings with the palm of your fretting hand instead of carefully damping them. As in #1, the thumb plays downstrokes, the fingers brush up.

Rural Blues Fingerpicking Pattern Rag Style #1 ◆3

Tempo: Moderate to fast shuffle

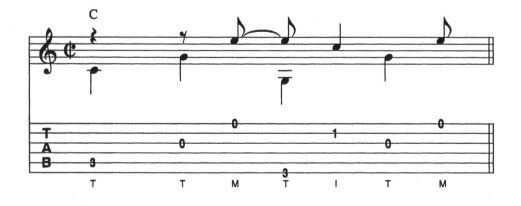

Fingerpicking blues guitarists Blind Blake, Willie McTell, Mance Lipscomb, Mississippi John Hurt, Blind Boy Fuller, Furry Lewis, and Gary Davis are often called "ragtime blues" players because their bouncy, rhythmic style seems to come from the popular ragtime dance music of the early part of the twentieth century. They all played a steady alternating thumb/bass, as in the previous pattern. Classic tunes in the style include "That Will Never Happen No More" (Blind Blake), "Warm It Up to Me" (Willie McTell), and "Candy Man" (John Hurt). Rockers who have played in this style include Eric Clapton (as in "Can't Find My Way Back Home") and the Rolling Stones ("It's All Over Now").

Rural Blues Fingerpicking Pattern Rag Style #2 ◆3

Tempo: Moderate to fast shuffle

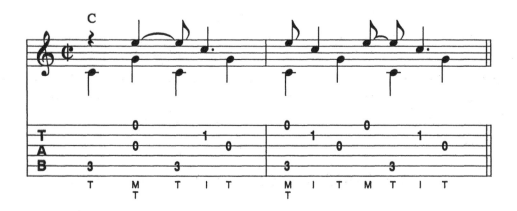

This is one of many possible variations of #1. For more possibilities, see the *Travis-Style Fingerpicking Patterns* in the **COUNTRY** section. Merle Travis' style was derived from this rural blues genre.

Rural Blues Fingerpicking Pattern Texas Style #1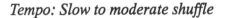

Tempo: Slow to moderate shuffle

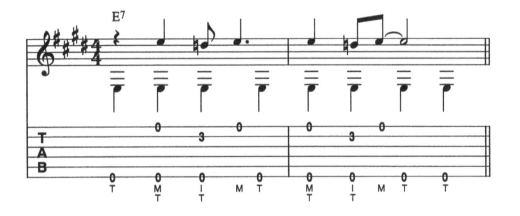

Lightnin' Hopkins popularized this fingerpicking blues style in which the thumb thumps out a steady bass on every downbeat, instead of alternating bass notes, while the fingers pick melody or rhythmic fills on the treble strings. Many of the players noted for this style (Big Bill Broonzy, John Lee Hooker, and Brownie McGhee) are not from Texas, but they all share the same rhythmic feel, as in "Key To The Highway" (McGhee, Eric Clapton, and others) and "I Wonder When" (Broonzy, Muddy Waters).

Rural Blues Fingerpicking Pattern Texas Style #2 ◆

Tempo: Slow shuffle

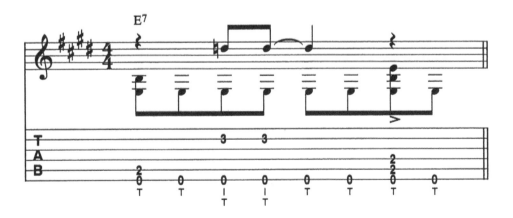

This is a slower version of the *Texas Style #1* pattern, as in "It Hurts Me Too" (Broonzy, Elmore James, and others) and "How Long Blues" (various artists). The steady, thumb bass plays two notes per downbeat, as in *ba-bump, ba-bump, ba-bump, ba-bump.*

"Hoochie Coochie Man" Blues Lick #1 ◆5

Tempo: Slow to moderately fast shuffle

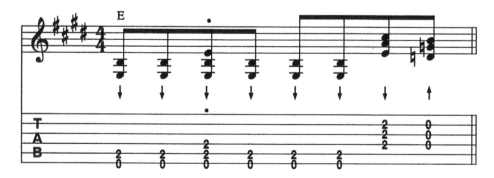

This popular blues lick is associated with the tune "Hoochie Coochie Man" (Muddy Waters) and "I'm a Man" (Bo Diddley).

"Hoochie Coochie Man" Blues Lick #2 ◆5

Tempo: Slow to moderately fast shuffle

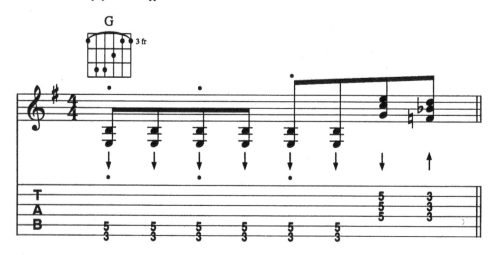

This is the same lick as *"Hoochie Coochie Man" Blues Lick #1*, made moveable. It's based on the barred E chord formation.

"Hoochie Coochie Man" Blues Lick #3 ◆5

Tempo: Moderate to fast shuffle

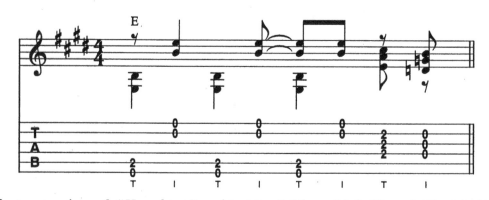

A faster version of *"Hoochie Coochie Man" Blues Lick #1* and *#2*, this lick includes thumb/downstrokes and finger/upstrokes. As in "Bad to the Bone" (George Thorogood).

Fingerpicking Boogie Lick #1

Tempo: Moderate to fast shuffle

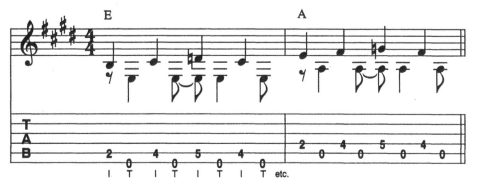

Suitable for "Boogie Chillun" and "Baby Please Don't Go" grooves, this and the next lick were often played by rockabilly guitarists in boogie tunes like "Matchbox" and "Blue Suede Shoes" (Carl Perkins). The index finger plays the higher of the two bass strings, the thumb plays the lower.

Fingerpicking Boogie Lick #2

Tempo: Moderate to fast shuffle

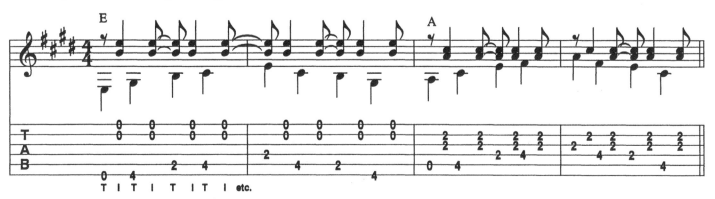

This is the same as #1, but the thumb starts it. The thumb plays bass, the index finger brushes up on the treble strings.

Basic Boogie Lick #1

Tempo: Slow to fast shuffle

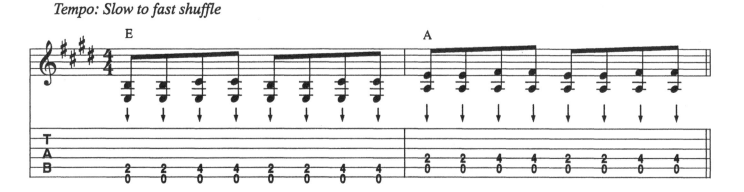

This archetypal boogie backup lick is usually played with the thumb or a flatpick. It's all down-strokes. It's for slow tunes like "Caress Me Baby" and "Honest I Do" (Jimmy Reed), to moderate and fast songs like "Don't Start Me Talkin'" (Sonny Boy Williamson), "Dust My Broom" (Elmore James and many others), "Farther On Up the Road" (Eric Clapton), and "Say What?" (Stevie Ray Vaughan).

Basic Boogie Lick (Moveable) ◆7

Tempo: Slow to fast shuffle

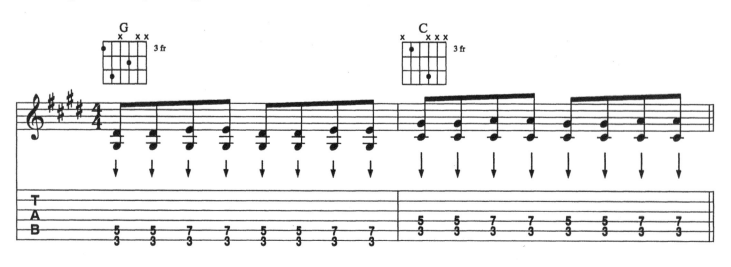

This is the same as the *Basic Boogie Lick*, but made moveable, based on abbreviated versions of the barred E and A chord formations. (Moveable chords or licks use only fretted, not open, strings; therefore, they can be played all over the fretboard.)

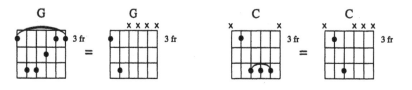

Boogie/Rock Lick #1 ◆8

Tempo: Moderate rock

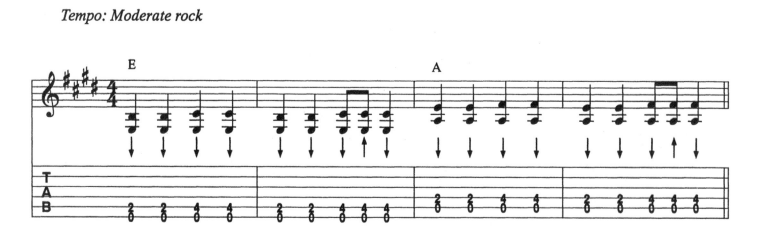

This is the strum for "Big Boss Man" (Jimmy Reed, Elvis Presley, and many others), "Good Morning Little Schoolgirl" (Sonny Boy Williamson), "Memphis Tennessee" (Chuck Berry), and "Smokestack Lightning" (Howlin' Wolf). It's the same as the *Rock/Boogie* strums of the **ROCK** section, but simplified slightly.

Boogie/Rock Lick (Moveable)

Tempo: Moderate rock

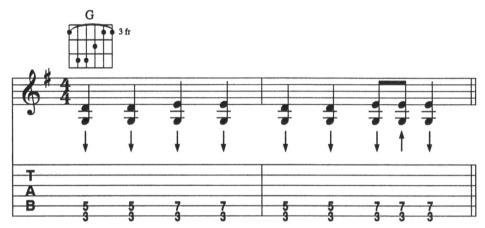

The moveable version of the *Boogie/Rock Lick* is based on the same chord formations as *Basic Boogie Lick (Moveable)*.

Boogie/Rock Lick #2 ⬩9⬩

Tempo: Moderate rock

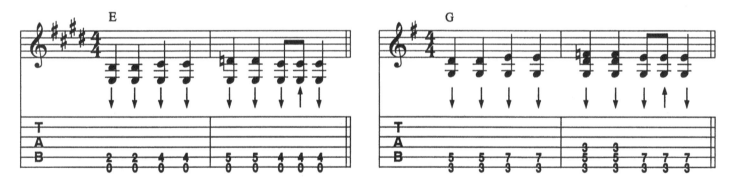

This is a variation of *Boogie/Rock Lick #1*. Here are the first position and moveable versions. You can play the same lick "up one string," i.e., on an A chord or a barred, abbreviated A chord.

Urban Blues Comping #1 ⬩10⬩

Tempo: Moderate to fast shuffle beat

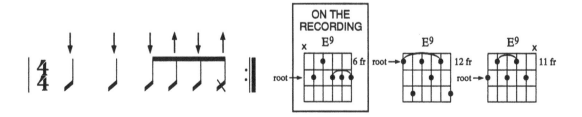

NOTE: These 9th chords are often used in all the *Urban Blues* patterns.

"Comping" is a swing/jazz expression for strumming backup chords, and it describes what the rhythm guitarist often does in a large electric blues band with a horn section (e.g., B. B. King's band). The chords are usually moveable and can be damped with the fretting hand. This strum is appropriate for tunes like "Everyday I Have the Blues" (B.B. King, Lowell Fulson, and many others), "Kansas City" (Wilbert Harrison and others), "One Bourbon, One Scotch, One Beer" (John Lee Hooker, George Thorogood), and "Eyesight to the Blind" (Sonny Boy Williamson, The Who, Eric Clapton).

Urban Blues Comping #2

Tempo: Slow to fast shuffle beat

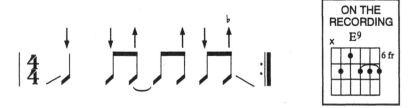

This is a variation of *Urban Blues Comping #1*. You can combine the two to make a two-bar pattern. The flat sign (♭) over the last stroke of this pattern tells you to play that chord a fret lower than the others and slide up a fret for the next stroke. The pattern works with or without this embellishment. Besides the tunes mentioned for *Urban Blues Comping #1*, this pattern works for slow tunes like "Stormy Monday Blues" (T-Bone Walker, Bobby Blue Bland), "Sweet Little Angel," and "Three O'Clock in the Morning" (B. B. King).

Urban Blues Comping #3 11

Tempo: Moderate to fast shuffle beat

This rhythm figure is played often by horns and guitar in tunes like "Rock Around the Clock" (Bill Haley and the Comets) and "Shake, Rattle and Roll" (Bill Haley, Joe Turner, and others). It's a swing band riff that crossed over into rock and roll, and it works as a backup comping pattern as well.

Urban Blues Comping #4

Tempo: Fast shuffle

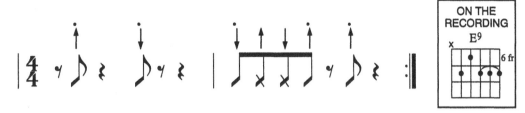

This is a faster variation of *Urban Blues Comping #3,* as in "Eyesight to the Blind" (mentioned before) and "Stang's Swang" (Stevie Ray Vaughan).

Slow Urban Blues Strum (6/8) 12

Tempo: Slow shuffle

This works with the blues tunes mentioned in *Urban Blues Comping #2.* More titles are: "Reconsider Baby" (Lowell Fulson and others), "Blues With a Feeling" (Little Walter, Paul Butterfield).

Slow Urban Blues Strum #2 12

Tempo: Slow to moderate

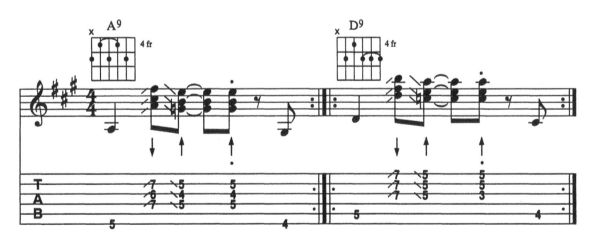

This strum is used for the tunes mentioned in *Slow Urban Blues Comping #1* and *Slow Urban Blues Comping #2.* These two sliding licks are often heard in Chicago-style blues bands. They are based on the 9th chords so often played in that genre. They are played usually on electric guitar.

Cross-References

By the mid 1960s, it was not unusual for electric blues players to use **ROCK** and **R&B/FUNK/SOUL** grooves or patterns. B.B. King's hits, "Why I Sing the Blues" and "The Thrill Is Gone," and Albert King's "Born Under a Bad Sign" are examples. Contemporary blues artists also use boogie patterns from the **ROCK** chapter, which are a bit fancier than those found in the **BLUES** chapter, and 6/8 strums from the **ROCK** and **R&B/FUNK/SOUL** chapters. A slow version of "Stormy Monday" could use one of these!

ROCK Chapter: *Rock Boogie #1 to #3, Rock Boogie Variation, Rock Boogie Shuffle #1 and #2, 6/8 Rock Strum #1 and #2.*

R&B/FUNK/SOUL Chapter: *Basic Sparse Soul/Rock Strum #1 to #6, Basic Soul/Rock Strum #1 to #4, Uptight Funk #3 and #4, Sliding Funk Pattern #1 and #2, Funk Ballad #1 to #3, Soul Shuffle #1 and #2, Soul 6/8 Time #1 to #3.*

ROCK

At its inception in the early 1950s, "rock" meant many things: rockabilly (a white Southern blend of R&B and honky-tonk country music); R&B, with honking saxes and a boogie beat; doo-wop (the intricate vocal harmonizing style invented by black and white urban street corner singing groups); and pop–the name reserved for everything else, usually lacking the strong beat of the other styles. Rock has expanded over the decades to include many more musical influences. As rock has grown, the guitar has become more prominent, and many electric and acoustic guitar styles have evolved.

The strums and picking patterns that follow apply to early Chuck Berry boogie woogie, country rock, folk rock, the harder-edged strumming of the Stones or Bon Jovi, Southern rock, Beatles-style and contemporary rock ballads, funk-rock, reggae, Latin rock, and more. As in the **BLUES** chapter, play all the patterns on electric and acoustic guitars. They are played both ways in rock recordings.

Basic Rock #1

Tempo: Fast or medium rock

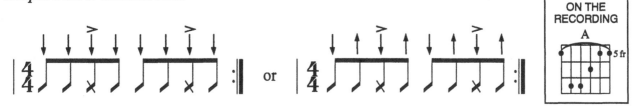

All downstrokes

This is the basic hard rock beat as in "I Want to Hold Your Hand" (the Beatles), "Every Breath You Take" (Police), "Beat It" (Michael Jackson), "Bad Medicine" (Bon Jovi), "Mony Mony" (Tommy James and the Shondells, Billy Idol), "Jump" (Van Halen), and "With or Without You" (U2).

Alternating up- and downstrokes

This has a slightly more relaxed rock feel, as in "Proud Mary" (Creedence Clearwater Revival [the Ike & Tina Turner version would be better with all downstrokes]), "Brown-Eyed Girl" (Van Morrison), "I'm a Believer" (the Monkees), and "Got My Mind Set on You" (George Harrison).

Basic Rock #2

Tempo: Fast or medium rock

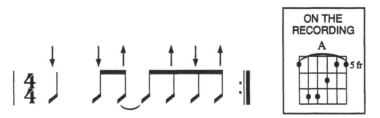

This has a looser, lighter feel than *Basic Rock #1* and is used often in country rock. Some examples are "American Pie" (Don McLean), "La Bamba" (Richie Valens, Los Lobos), "Solitary Man" (Neil Diamond), "Maggie May" (Rod Stewart), "Kokomo" and "Sloop John B." (the Beach Boys), and "Time After Time" (Cyndi Lauper).

Tempo: Moderately slow to moderate rock

This is for rock with a slightly funky feel, as in "You're No Good" (Linda Ronstadt, Betty Everett), "I Heard It Through the Grapevine" (Marvin Gaye [the Creedence Clearwater Revival version sounds more like *Basic Rock #1* with alternating up and downstrokes]), "It's Too Late" (Carole King), and "Sittin' on the Dock of the Bay" (Otis Redding, Michael Bolton).

Rock Shuffle #1 ⬥15

Tempo: Moderate to bright shuffle

This basic shuffle strum fits tunes like "Bad, Bad Leroy Brown" (Jim Croce), "Pride and Joy"(Stevie Ray Vaughan), "All Shook Up" (Elvis Presley), "Crazy Little Thing Called Love" (Queen), "California Girls" (Beach Boys), "Higher Ground" (Stevie Wonder, Red Hot Chili Peppers). On tunes with moderate tempos, you can use all downstrokes to give this strum a harder edge.

Rock Shuffle #2 ⬥15

Tempo: Moderate shuffle

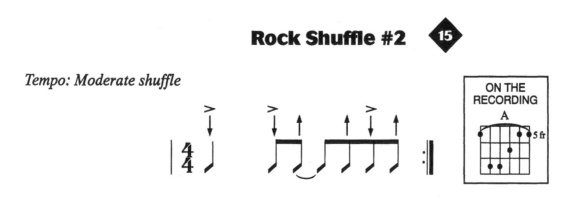

This is the same as *Country Strum #2*, as in "Chains" (the Cookies, the Beatles), "Mountain of Love" (Harold Dorman, Johnny Rivers), "How Sweet It Is (To Be Loved By You)" (Marvin Gaye, James Taylor), "Loves Me Like a Rock" and "Slip Slidin' Away" (Paul Simon).

Fast Rock Shuffle

Tempo: Fast shuffle

The same as *Country Strum #1,* this is the rhythm strum for rockabilly classics like "That's All Right, Mama," "Mystery Train" and "My Baby Left Me" (Elvis Presley), "Mrs. Robinson" (Simon and Garfunkel), and "Mother's Little Helper" (Rolling Stones). It's usually played on an acoustic guitar.

Rock Boogie #1 ⑰

Tempo: Moderately slow to fast rock

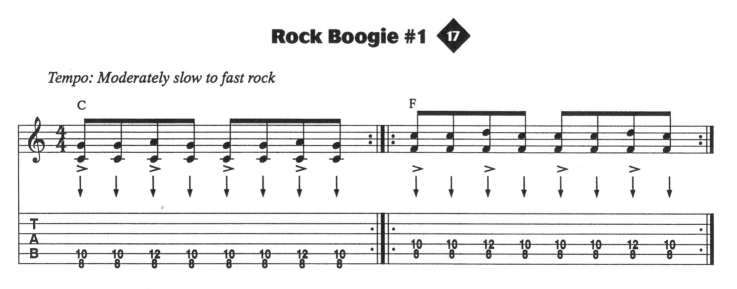

Popularized by Chuck Berry, this is a variation of *Blues Boogie #1.* It's based on the barred E7 and A7 chords (see *Basic Boogie Lick [Moveable]* for more explanation). It was used in countless fifties rock tunes and is still a favorite today: "Mony Mony" (Tommy James and the Shondells, Billy Idol), "Johnny B. Goode" (Chuck Berry), "Get Back" (the Beatles), and "Honky Tonk Women" (the Rolling Stones).

Rock Boogie #1 Variation ⑰

Tempo: Moderately slow to fast rock

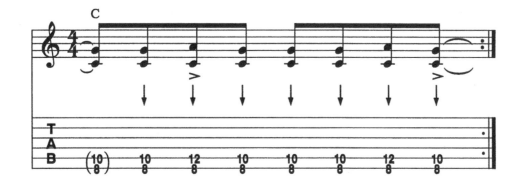

This is the same as *Rock Boogie #1,* but the first beat is anticipated to make the strum more syncopated. Mix the two patterns together.

Rock Boogie #2

Tempo: Moderately slow to fast rock

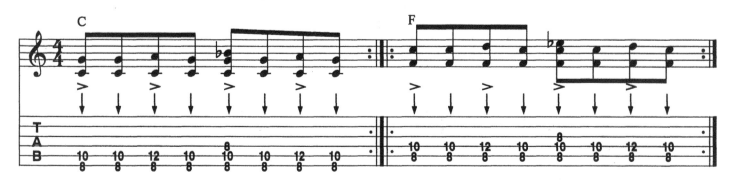

This is used in the same types of tunes as the other two *Rock Boogie* strums. For still more variation, anticipate the first beat by tying it to the last beat, as in *Rock Boogie #1, Variation*.

Rock Boogie #3

Tempo: Moderately slow to fast rock

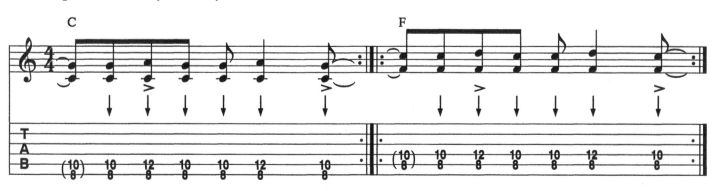

This is yet another syncopated variation of *Rock Boogie #1*.

Rock Boogie Shuffle #1 19

Tempo: Moderately slow to fast shuffle

This is similar to the *Moveable Blues Boogie Shuffle*. It has a relaxed feel when you alternate down and upstrokes, as in "Blue Suede Shoes" (Carl Perkins, Elvis Presley) and "It's Still Rock and Roll to Me" (Billy Joel), and a more driving rhythm when you only play downstrokes, as in "Sweet Little Sixteen" (Chuck Berry) and "That'll Be the Day" (Buddy Holly).

Rock Boogie Shuffle #2

Tempo: Moderately slow to fast shuffle

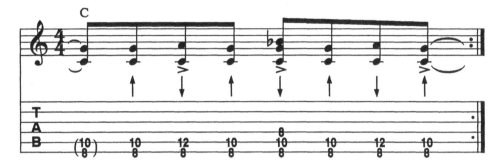

This is more syncopated than *Rock Boogie Shuffle #1*. You can also play "straight" (without the anticipated first beat) and add the anticipation occasionally for variety and to give the rhythm an extra push. "Your Mama Don't Dance" (Loggins and Messina), "Some Kind of Wonderful" (Grand Funk), and "Rockin' Robin" (Bobby Day, Michael Jackson) are some examples.

Fast Rock Strum 21

Tempo: Fast rock

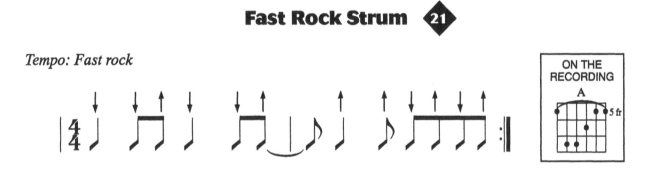

This is a two-bar pattern for tunes like "Good Lovin" (Rascals), "Turn on Your Love Light" (Bobby Bland), "The Doctor" (Doobie Brothers), and "I'm a Believer" (the Monkees).

Bo Diddley-Style Strum #1 22

Tempo: Bright rock

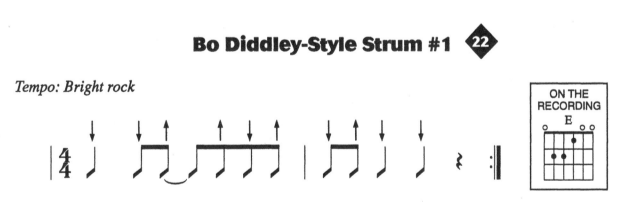

There are many variations of this strum, which is identified with Bo Diddley. Tunes with this rhythm groove include "Bo Diddley" and "Mona" (Bo Diddley), "Not Fade Away" (Buddy Holly), "Faith" (George Michael), "Willie and the Hand Jive" (Johnny Otis, Eric Clapton), and "Magic Carpet Ride" (Steppenwolf).

EQUIPMENT NOTE: Bo Diddley played electric guitar with a lot of reverb and tremolo, so these effects are used often with this strum.

Bo Diddley-Style Strum #2

Tempo: Bright rock

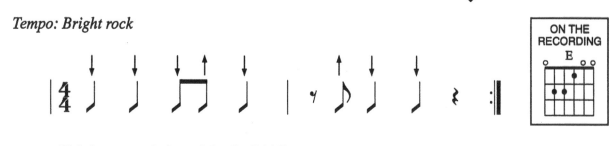

This is one variation of the Bo Diddley groove.

"Hi-Heel Sneakers" Boogie/Rock Strum #1 ㉓

Tempo: Moderate to bright rock

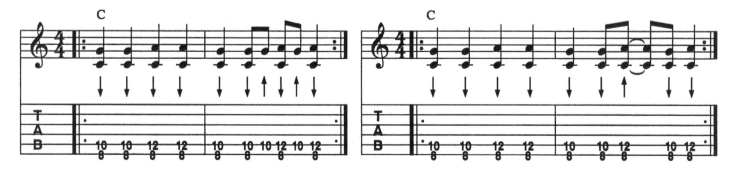

"Hi-Heel Sneakers" (Tommy Tucker) was such a popular bar-band tune that its rhythm groove became known as the "Hi-Heel Sneakers" beat. As in "Lay Down Sally" (Eric Clapton), "Bread And Butter" (the Newbeats), "Cold As Ice" (Foreigner), "Morning Train (Nine To Five)" (Sheena Easton). Here are two variations of the groove, the second a bit more syncopated than the first.

"Hi-Heel Sneakers" Boogie/Rock Strum #2 ㉓

Tempo: Moderate to bright rock

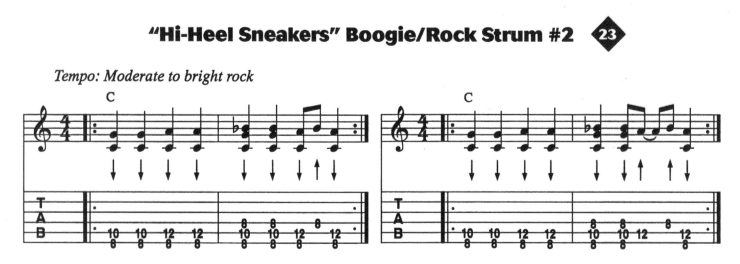

This is the same as *#1*, but a bit bluesier with the flatted 7th note added, as in "Memphis, Tennessee" (Chuck Berry, Johnny Rivers), "Freeze Frame" (J. Geils Band), "Can I Get a Witness" (Marvin Gaye, Rolling Stones), "The Boy From New York City" (the Newbeats, Manhattan Transfer).

"Hi-Heel Sneakers" Rock Strum #1 ◆24◆

Tempo: Moderate to bright rock

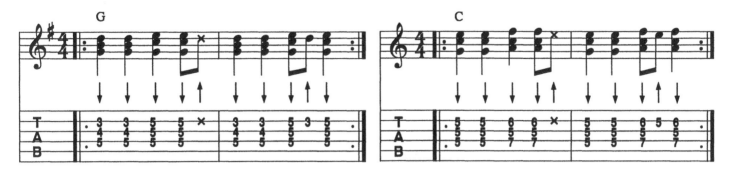

This is the same as the *"Hi-Heel Sneakers" Boogie/Rock Strum #1,* but with chords instead of the bass-note boogie lick. The three chord shapes used in this pattern can be fattened by adding first string notes:

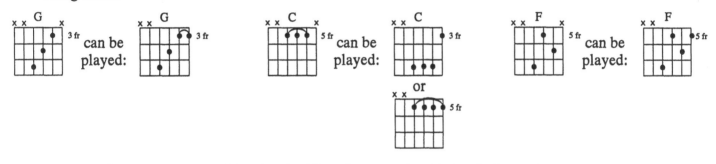

This strum is moveable: that is, like all strums in this book, it can be played in any key. Consider the G chord, an abbreviated "barred E" chord; the C chord is an abbreviated "barred A":

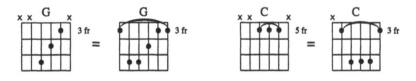

"Hi-Heel Sneakers" Rock Strum #2 ◆24◆

Tempo: Moderate to bright rock

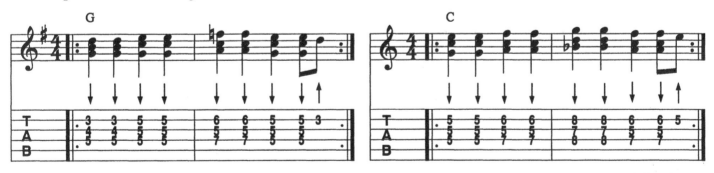

This is the same as *"Hi-Heel Sneakers" Boogie/Rock Strum #2,* with chords instead of the bass-note boogie lick. For a still brighter sound, play these chords:

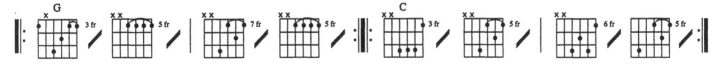

Rock/Funk #1

Tempo: Bright rock/funk

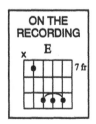

This is suitable for fast, strum-filled tunes like the Doobie Brothers' "Listen to the Music" and "Long Train Running" or Bachman-Turner Overdrive's "You Ain't Seen Nothing Yet" and "Let It Ride."

Rock/Funk #2

Tempo: Moderate to bright rock/funk

This is rhythmically tighter than *Rock/Funk #1*, as in "Centerfold" (J. Geils Band), "After Midnight" (Eric Clapton), "I Love Rock 'n' Roll" (Joan Jett), "Spinning Wheel" (Blood, Sweat & Tears), and "Purple Haze" (Jimi Hendrix). The first bar is the main groove of this strum. The second bar is optional and can be played every other time (as written) or at the end of a musical phrase or when there is a space between lyrics.

EQUIPMENT NOTE: Often played on electric guitar with a lot of distortion.

Rock/Funk #3

Tempo: Moderately slow and heavy rock/funk

This is for slower tempos, as in "Wild Thing" (the Troggs, Jimi Hendrix), "Hey Joe" (Hendrix, the Leaves), "Sgt. Pepper's Lonely Hearts Club Band" and "She Came in Through the Bathroom Window" (the Beatles). As in *Rock/Funk #2*, you can play the first bar most of the time and throw in bar two occasionally.

EQUIPMENT NOTE: Often played on electric guitar with a lot of distortion.

Rock/Funk #4

Tempo: Moderate to bright rock/funk

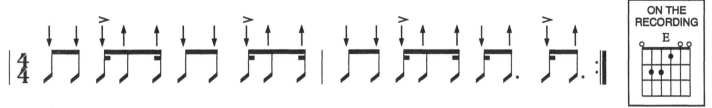

There are countless ways to vary *Rock/Funk #2* and *#3*. This syncopated version fits tunes like "Sweet Home Alabama" (Lynyrd Skynyrd) and "Magic Man" (Heart).

EQUIPMENT NOTE: Often played on electric guitar with a lot of distortion.

6/8 Rock Strum #1

Tempo: Moderately slow rock ballad

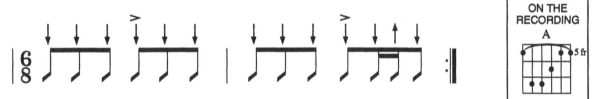

You can use the first bar and occasionally add the second bar for variety, or you can alternate the two bars as written. This strum fits countless fifties ballads like "Oh Donna" (Richie Valens), "To Know Him Is to Love Him" (Teddy Bears, Peter and Gordon, Bobby Vinton), and "You Send Me" (Sam Cooke).

EQUIPMENT NOTE: Often played on electric guitar with reverb.

6/8 Rock Strum #2

Tempo: Slow rock ballad

For slower 6/8 tunes like "Sleepwalk" (Santo and Johnny), "When a Man Loves a Woman" (Percy Sledge), "Time Is on My Side" (Wilson Pickett, the Rolling Stones), "This Boy" and "Oh Darling" (the Beatles), "Red House" (Jimi Hendrix), and "House of the Rising Sun" (the Animals). As in *6/8 Rock Strum #1,* you can use just the first bar and play the second bar occasionally, or you can alternate the two.

EQUIPMENT NOTE: Often played on electric guitar with reverb.

Tempo: Moderately slow rock ballad

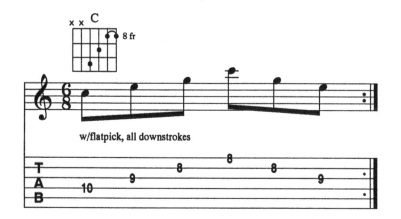

w/flatpick, all downstrokes

Use for the same tunes as the *6/8 Rock Strums*. To play an arpeggio, pick the notes of a chord in rapid, even succession. This picking pattern was especially popular in early rock ballads like "The Great Pretender" (the Platters) and "Young Love" (Tab Hunter, Sonny James). The guitar plays first position or moveable chords.

EQUIPMENT NOTE: In early rock, this lick was usually played on an electric guitar that was drenched in reverb and tremolo. More recently, chorus, phase shifter, and flanger have been used. (See **EQUIPMENT APPENDIX** for description of these effects.)

6/8 Rock Arpeggio #2

Tempo: Slow to moderately slow rock ballad

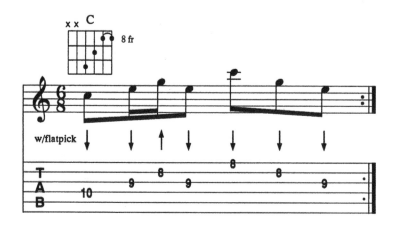

w/flatpick

This works well in the same tunes as *6/8 Rock Strum #2*. It has more rhythmic bounce than *6/8 Rock Arpeggio #1*.

EQUIPMENT NOTE: The same as *6/8 Rock Arpeggio #1*.

Reggae Strum #1

Tempo: Moderate rock

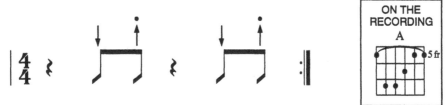

The electric guitar usually plays very sparse, clipped rhythm strums in reggae music. The tone is very sharp and biting. To achieve that clipped effect, moveable chord fragments are often employed. They are easier to mute (with the fretting hand), as in "The Harder They Come" (Jimmy Cliff), "Stir It Up" (Bob Marley and the Wailers), and "I Shot the Sheriff" (Bob Marley and the Wailers, Eric Clapton).

EQUIPMENT NOTE: To get the appropriate biting tone, use the back (treble) pickup on an electric guitar.

Reggae Strum #2

Tempo: Moderate rock

This is the same as *Reggae Strum #1,* but even sparser.

Reggae Strum #3

Tempo: Moderate rock

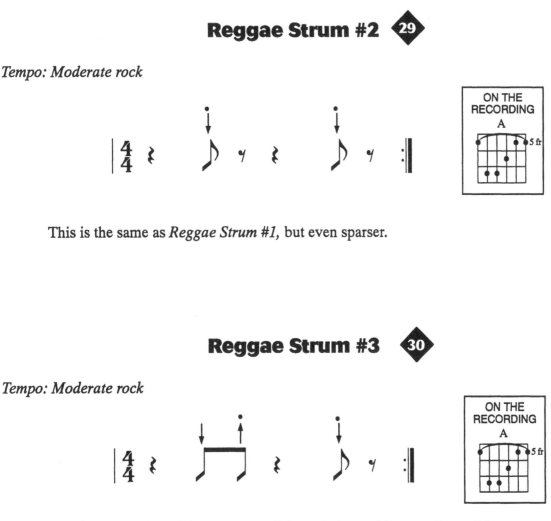

This is yet another of the many possible variations of *Reggae Strum #1.*

Latin Rock #1

Tempo: Moderate to fast Latin rock

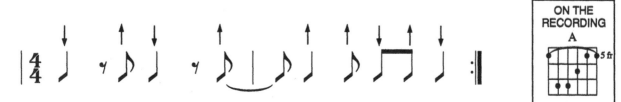

This bossa nova* beat resembles the *Fast Rock Strum.* As heard in "Along Comes Mary" (the Association), "You Are the Sunshine of My Life" (Stevie Wonder), and "I Say a Little Prayer for You" (Dionne Warwick, Aretha Franklin).

*NOTE: Bossa nova is a popular Brazilian dance music that has mingled with American jazz and pop.

Latin Rock #2

Tempo: Moderate Latin rock

For funkier, more percussive beats than *Latin Rock #1,* as in "Oye Como Va" and "Evil Ways" (Santana).

Latin Rock #3

Tempo: Moderately slow to moderate Latin rock

This is a gentler bossa nova strum, as in José Feliciano's version of "Light My Fire," "And I Love Her" (the Beatles), the "Theme from M.A.S.H. (Suicide Is Painless)," and bossa nova standards like "The Girl From Ipanema." At a slower tempo it works for "Killing Me Softly With His Song" (Roberta Flack).

Latin Rock #4

Tempo: Fast Latin rock

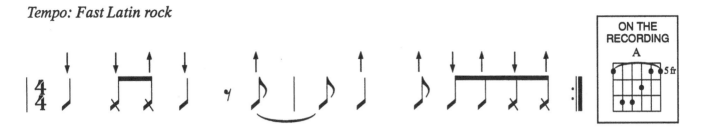

Similar to *Latin Rock #1,* but with some damped strums, this fast samba beat fits tunes like "(Marie's the Name) His Latest Flame" (Elvis Presley), "Love the One You're With," and "Suite: Judy Blue Eyes" (Crosby, Stills & Nash).

Latin Rock #5

Tempo: Moderately slow to moderately bright Latin rock

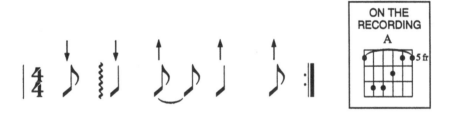

The wiggly line ( ) indicates a slow rake in which the flatpick hits one string at a time in rapid succession, like a quick arpeggio. This rhythm was popular in 1950s rock tunes like "Love Is Strange" (Mickey and Sylvia), "Diana" (Paul Anka), and "Little Darlin'" (the Diamonds). It also works in 1960s tunes like "Under the Boardwalk" (the Drifters), "It's Now or Never" (Elvis Presley), and "Stand By Me" (Ben E. King, John Lennon).

Fingerpicking Rock #1 (Swamp Rock) ◆34◆

Tempo: Moderately slow to moderate rock

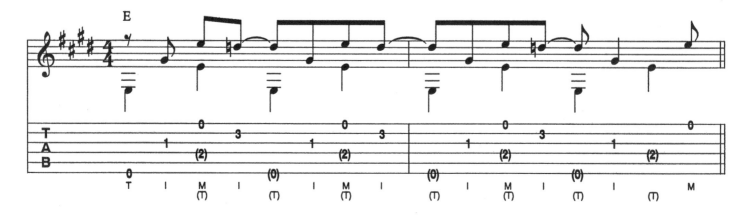

This fingerpicking pattern is appropriate for swamp rock tunes like "Born on the Bayou" (Creedence Clearwater Revival), "Polk Salad Annie" (Tony Joe White), and "Little Sister" (Elvis Presley, Dwight Yoakam). If you leave out the tablature numbers that are in parenthesis, you can easily adapt the pattern to a flatpick.

EQUIPMENT NOTE: Though this is an acoustic style, it sounds very funky on electric guitar.

Fingerpicking Rock #2 ◆34◆

Tempo: Moderately fast rock

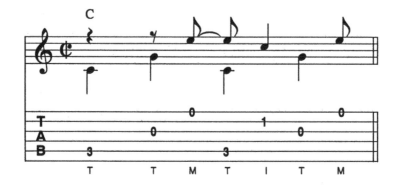

This cut time fingerpicking pattern works in tunes like "Dust in the Wind" (Kansas), "I Feel Fine" (the Beatles), and "It's All Over Now" (the Rolling Stones). It is the same as *Rural Blues Fingerpicking Rag Style #1.*

Fingerpicking Rock #3

Tempo: Moderate rock

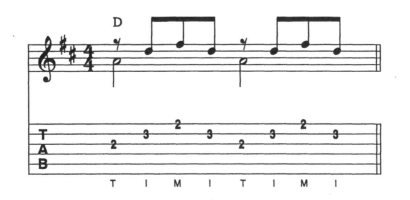

This simple pattern is a steady backup lick behind a straight rock beat, as in "Tired of Waiting for You" (the Kinks) and "Mama Told Me (Not to Come)" (Three Dog Night).

EQUIPMENT NOTE: Often played on electric guitar enhanced by flanger, chorus, or tremolo.

Fingerpicking Rock #4

Tempo: Moderate rock

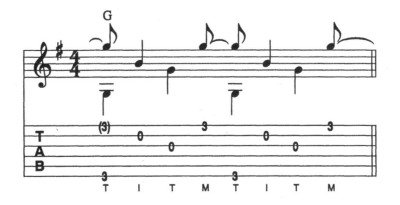

This folk-rock pattern resembles *Fingerpicking Rock #2,* but with a rock beat. As played in "Mr. Tambourine Man" (the Byrds), and "I Am a Rock" (Simon and Garfunkel).

EQUIPMENT NOTE: Often played on acoustic guitar, acoustic or electric twelve string, or electric six string enhanced by chorus or flanger.

Rockabilly Fingerpicking #1 36

Tempo: Moderate to fast shuffle

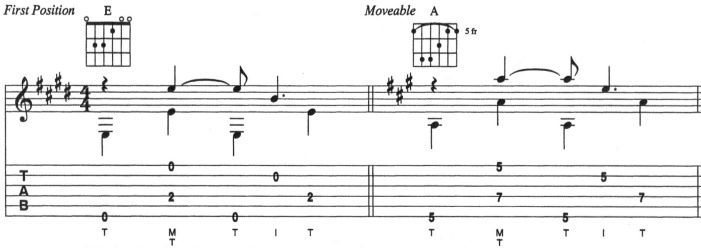

This is played in first position in the key of E. The key-of-A pattern next to it is the same lick, moved up five frets. It is based on a barred E chord. Move it up two frets, and it's a B lick; up one more fret, it's a C lick, etc.

This pattern and the other rockabilly patterns that follow can be heard in songs like "Blue Suede Shoes" (Carl Perkins, Elvis Presley), "That's All Right, Mama" and "Good Rockin' Tonight" (Elvis Presley), "Crazy Little Thing Called Love" (Queen), and "All My Loving" (the Beatles), as well as country hits like "My Baby Thinks He's a Train" (Roseanne Cash) and "Heartbroke" (Ricky Skaggs).

Rockabilly fingerpicking is based on the style of Merle Travis and Chet Atkins. Travis and Atkins embellished the raggy blues fingerpicking style of rural blues players and made their licks moveable (see *Rural Blues Fingerpicking, Rag Style* in the **BLUES** chapter). As in raggy blues, rockabilly patterns feature a steady, alternating thumb bass. Many rockabilly pickers simulate fingerpicking by playing the bass notes with a flatpick and the treble notes with the middle finger.

EQUIPMENT NOTE: All the *Rockabilly Fingerpicking* patterns sound good on acoustic or electric guitar, but for an authentic rockabilly sound, play an electric with a "slapback" echo effect (see **EQUIPMENT APPENDIX**).

Rockabilly Fingerpicking #2 36

Tempo: Moderate to fast shuffle

This is a variation of *Rockabilly Fingerpicking #1*. Use it as a repeated pattern or mix all four *Rockabilly Fingerpicking* patterns to make two-bar phrases.

Rockabilly Fingerpicking #3

Tempo: Moderate to fast shuffle

This is the same as *Rockabilly Fingerpicking #1,* with a hammer-on added. Try mixing it with #2.

EQUIPMENT NOTE: Same as *Rockabilly Fingerpicking #1.*

Rockabilly Fingerpicking #4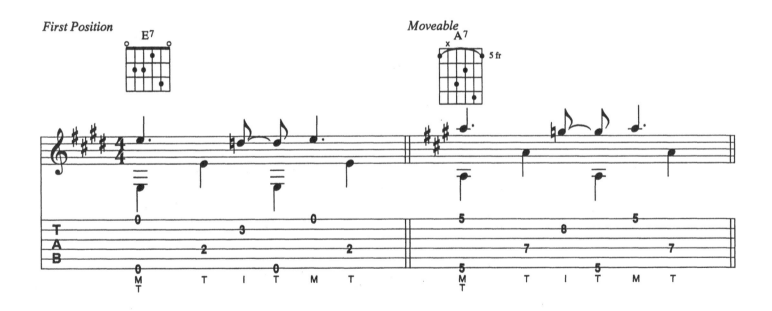

Tempo: Moderate to fast

This is yet another of the countless variations on this theme.

EQUIPMENT NOTE: Same as *Rockabilly Fingerpicking #1.*

Rockabilly Fingerpicking #5 ◆38

Tempo: Moderately fast

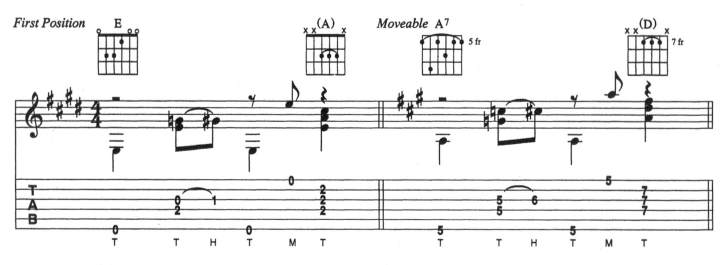

This pattern works well in faster rockabilly tunes like "Mystery Train" and "My Baby Left Me" (Elvis Presley), and country hits like "Workingman's Blues" (Merle Haggard) and "That's What I Like About You" (Trisha Yearwood). Fret the final barred chord of each pattern with your ring finger.

EQUIPMENT NOTE: Same as *Rockabilly Fingerpicking #1.*

Rock Ballad #1 ◆39

Tempo: Moderately slow rock

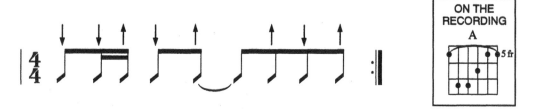

This is the same pattern as *Basic Rock #3*, only slower, as in "The Best of My Love" (the Eagles), "Right Time of the Night" (Jennifer Warnes), "Stand By Me" (Ben E. King, John Lennon), and "I'll Be There" (Jackson 5).

Rock Ballad #2 ◆39

Tempo: Slow rock

This is slower than *Rock Ballad #1,* as in "Hey Jude" and "Let It Be" (the Beatles), "Every Rose Has Its Thorn" (Poison), and "Everytime You Go Away" (Paul Young).

Rock Ballad #3

Tempo: Slower than Rock Ballad #2

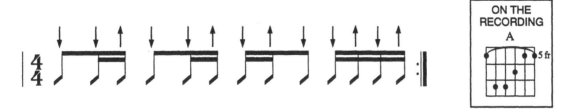

The slower the tempo, the more sixteenth-note strums are added, as in "Knockin' On Heaven's Door" (Bob Dylan, Eric Clapton), "Helpless" (Neil Young), and "Don't Know What You Got ('Till It's Gone)" (Cinderella).

Rock Ballad #4

Tempo: Same as Rock Ballad #2 or #3

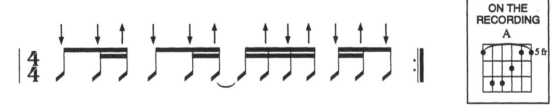

This is one of countless possible variations of the ROCK BALLAD #2 or #3 strums.

Fingerpicking Rock Ballad #1 41

Tempo: Slow to moderately slow rock ballad

There are many variations of this fingerpicking pattern. It's a typical backup for tunes like "You've Got a Friend" and "Candy Man" (James Taylor), and "I'll Have to Say I Love You in a Song" (Jim Croce).

EQUIPMENT NOTE: Use acoustic guitar, electric guitar enhanced by effects (echo, flanger, tremolo, chorus, etc.), or twelve-string guitar.

Fingerpicking Rock Ballad #2 ◆41◆

Tempo: Slow to moderately slow rock ballad

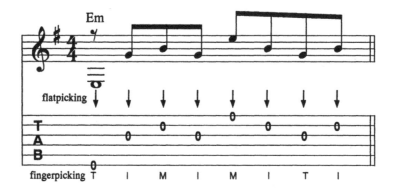

This is an alternative pattern to *Fingerpicking Rock Ballad #1*. It works in songs with the same type of beat, such as "Play With Fire" and "As Tears Go By" (the Rolling Stones) and "Lady" (Kenny Rogers).

EQUIPMENT NOTE: Same as *Fingerpicking Rock Ballad #1*.

Fingerpicking Rock Ballad #3 ◆42◆

Tempo: Slowly, with a half-time feel

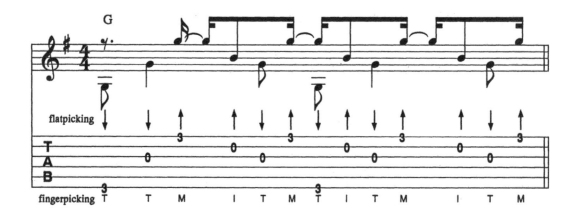

This one can also be played with a flatpick. It fits rock ballads like "Every Rose Has Its Thorn" (Poison), "Sailing" (Christopher Cross), "Fire and Rain" (James Taylor), "Killing Me Softly With His Song" (Roberta Flack), and "Knockin' on Heaven's Door" (Bob Dylan, Eric Clapton).

EQUIPMENT NOTE: Same as *Fingerpicking Rock Ballad #1*.

Fingerpicking Rock Ballad #4

Tempo: Very slow

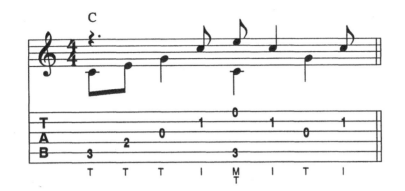

Similar to *Fingerpicking Rock Ballad #2,* this is for tunes like "Stairway to Heaven" (Led Zeppelin), "Let It Be Me" (the Everly Brothers) and "I'll Be There" (Jackson 5).

EQUIPMENT NOTE: Same as *Fingerpicking Rock Ballad #1.*

Cross-References

Rock borrows heavily from all musical forms. Often, it has used R&B/funk/soul rhythms, while contemporary techno-pop uses disco and uptight funk* patterns.

R&B/FUNK/SOUL Chapter: *Basic Sparse Soul/Rock Strum #1 to #5, Basic Soul/Rock Strum #1 to #4, Uptight Funk #1 to #6, Disco Scratch Rhythm #1 to #3.*

Rockabilly lead guitarists play many of the boogie licks found in the **BLUES** chapter. The same licks are staples of swamp rock and Southern rock. Rockabilly rhythm guitarists (especially acoustic guitarists) play Country strums; Chuck Berry played a bluegrass strum on electric guitar on his first hit, "Mabellene."

BLUES Chapter: *Rural Fingerpicking Blues Pattern (Texas Style) #1 and #2, Fingerpicking Boogie Lick #1 and #2.*

COUNTRY Chapter: *Bluegrass Strum #1 to #3, Country Strum #1 and #2, Honky Tonk Strum.*

Early rock was sometimes called "bop" (as Gene Vincent said, "Let's bop again, Blue Caps!"), and it borrowed the swing band comping found in the **BLUES** chapter. (For example, listen to Bill Haley's "Rock Around the Clock.")

BLUES Chapter: *Urban Blues Comping #1 to #4.*

Rock steals fingerpicking from blues (e.g., the Rolling Stones' "This Could Be the Last Time" and "It's All Over Now"), country, and folk (e.g., Kansas' folky "Dust in the Wind").

BLUES Chapter: *Rural Blues Fingerpicking Pattern (Rag Style) #1 and #2*

FOLK Chapter: *Folk Fingerpicking #1 and #2.*

* Rhythms found in this book.

R&B/FUNK/SOUL

It has been called R&B (rhythm and blues), funk, soul, and many other names. In spite of musical crossover and racial and musical integration (e.g., super funkmeister George Clinton produced the white rock group, the Red Hot Chili Peppers), there are still "soul" (read "African American") radio, "soul" video programming, and "soul" charts . . . and a "soul" section in your local record store. As the strums that follow illustrate, "black" pop music has a funkier beat than "white" pop music. Here are some other qualities that set it apart for the guitarist:

- Funk strums are more rhythmically complex than rock strums because the beat is more subdivided. Notice that there are many sixteenth-note strums in the patterns that follow. To give definition to those rapid sixteenth-note patterns, a crisp sharp-toned electric guitar has always been preferable. The Fender Stratocaster and Telecaster have long been standard funk guitars, though many modern hybrid electrics can achieve the same sound.

- Moveable chords are the chords of choice, because they can be muted more easily than first-position chords. Muting is needed for the same reason a sharp-toned electric guitar is used: it gives sharp definition to those sixteenth-note strums.

- In rock and metal, the beat is often guitar-driven. A raunchy guitar riff defines the groove, and the bass and drums follow that riff. In soul or funk music, the bass and drums are more likely to define the rhythmic feel, and the guitar responds to them.

- Space is important in funk patterns. Notice how the patterns that follow often contain "holes," rather than constant strumming. This can push and syncopate the beat. To make up syncopated funk patterns, listen to conga drummers and try to imitate their rhythmic approach.

Basic Sparse Soul/Rock Strum #1　🔶43

Tempo: Moderately slow to fast rock

Like one of the most basic reggae beats, this strum is played in a high register and highlights the snare drum accents. It was used in many early soul tunes, such as "In the Midnight Hour" (Wilson Pickett), and "Ain't too Proud to Beg" (the Temptations).

Basic Sparse Soul/Rock Strum #2

Tempo: Slow to moderate rock/ballad

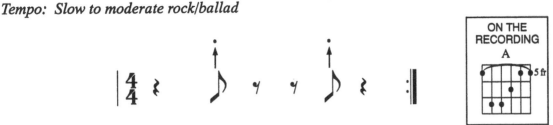

A more syncopated version of the previous strum was used in early soul/rock ballads like "Stand By Me" (Ben E. King) and "Under the Boardwalk" (the Drifters).

Basic Sparse Soul/Rock Strum #3

Tempo: Slow to moderate rock

This is a slight variation of #2, as in "Walk On By" (Dionne Warwick).

Basic Sparse Soul/Rock Strum #4

Tempo: Moderate to fast rock

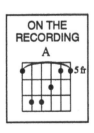

This is another more syncopated variation of #1 and #2.

Basic Sparse Soul/Rock Strum #5

Tempo: Moderate to fast rock

This is still another syncopated variation. All of these can be mixed and matched, and two-bar patterns can be created (i.e., play #2 followed by #4).

Basic Sparse Soul/Rock Strum #6

Tempo: Moderate rock

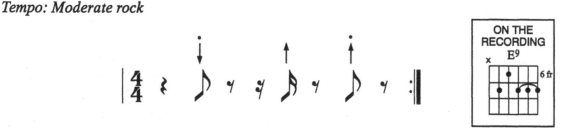

This strum has a funkier feel than the other *Sparse Soul/Rock Strums*. The sixteenth note adds syncopation. It has a rhythmic feel similar to the Sam and Dave hits, "Hold On, I'm Comin'" and "Soul Man."

Basic Soul/Rock Strum #1

Tempo: Moderate to fast rock

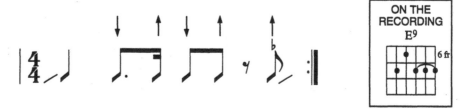

This strum is played in soul classics like "Papa's Got a Brand New Bag" and "I Feel Good" (James Brown), "Knock On Wood" (Eddie Floyd and many others), and "Mustang Sally" (Wilson Pickett). The last stroke is played one fret lower and slides up a fret, so that the first beat of the repeated pattern is a slide. The strum also works well without this extra feature.

Basic Soul/Rock Strum #2

Tempo: Moderate to fast rock

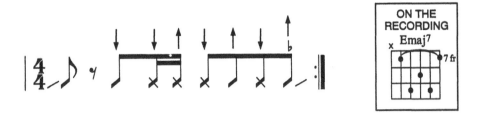

This is the same as #1, with a slightly funkier feel (because of the extra "scratch" strokes), as in "She's Lookin' Good" (Wilson Pickett). If a strum includes many muted strokes, it is sometimes called a "scratch rhythm."

Basic Soul/Rock Strum #3

Tempo: Moderate rock ballad to moderate rock

This is a slower variation of #1, for tunes like "Let's Stay Together" (Al Green), "Midnight Train to Georgia" (Gladys Knight and the Pips), "The Thrill Is Gone" (B.B. King), and "Just My Imagination" (the Temptations, the Rolling Stones).

Basic Soul/Rock Strum #3 (Variation)

Tempo: Moderate rock ballad to moderate rock

This is the same as #3, with one variation: the last beat is tied to the first, which creates a very syncopated feel. Try alternating #3 and #4, so that the "anticipated first beat" happens every other bar.

Basic Soul/Rock Strum #4

Tempo: Moderate to fast rock

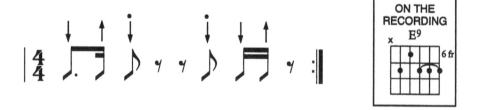

This strum fits songs like "Shotgun" (Junior Walker) or "Respect," "Think," and "Baby I Love You" (Aretha Franklin). Note all the "space" in this pattern.

Uptight Funk #1

Tempo: Moderate to fast rock

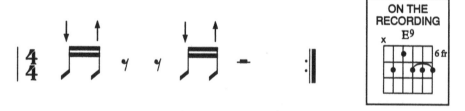

James Brown popularized this "uptight" (funky/high tension) feel in a series of tunes like "Say It Loud–I'm Black and I'm Proud," "I Got the Feeling," and "Ain't It Funky Now." Though each tune had a different guitar part, the overall groove was the same. His arranging in the late 1960s pushed soul music in a much funkier "rhythm groove" direction.

Uptight Funk #2

Tempo: Moderate funk

This is the flip side of *Uptight Funk #1,* which had few strokes and a lot of space. Here, you achieve the same groove with a scratch rhythm (many sixteenth-note strums), as in James Brown's "Cold Sweat" and "There Was a Time."

Uptight Funk #3

Tempo: Moderate funk

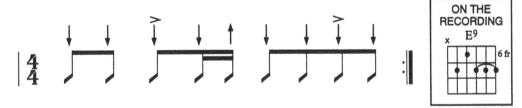

This is a modern funk strum, as in "I Give You My Heart" (Baby Face), "It's Gonna Be Alright" (Aaron Hall), and "Disappear" (INXS).

Uptight Funk #4

Tempo: Moderate funk

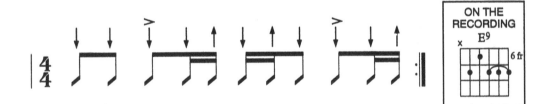

This is one of many ways to vary *#3*, as in "Don't Wanna Love You" (Shanice) and "Hold On" (En Vogue).

Uptight Funk #5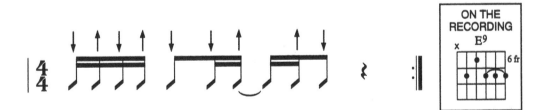

Tempo: Moderate funk

This is another modern funk groove. It has more sixteenth notes, as in "Seven Day Weekend" (Grace Jones).

Uptight Funk #6

Tempo: Moderate funk

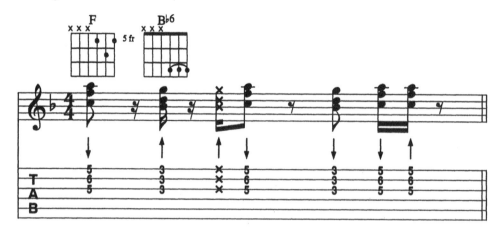

This is an "uptight funk" beat that manipulates space and shifting chords. The chord shapes are abbreviated, three-note or four-note formations to make the rapid shifting easier. When you make up variations on this theme, use any closely related chords, such as I and IV (e.g., E and A), I and V (E and B), or I and ii (E and F#m). Early examples of this style of strum include "Want Ads" and "Stick-Up" (the Honey Cone), and "Clean Up Woman" (Betty Wright).

Sliding Funk Pattern #1 52

Tempo: Moderate funk ballad to fast funk

The slides are part of the rhythm of this pattern. Slide the whole chord down a fret, then slide back up to normal position, then down, then up again, all on the strength of one stroke of the pick. The pattern also works without slides. As in Isaac Hayes' "Do Your Thing," and "Thank You (Falettinme Be Mice Elf Agin)" (Sly and the Family Stone).

Sliding Funk Pattern #2 52

Tempo: Moderate funk ballad to fast funk

This is a variation of *Sliding Funk Pattern #1*.

Sliding Funk Pattern #3

Tempo: Moderate funk

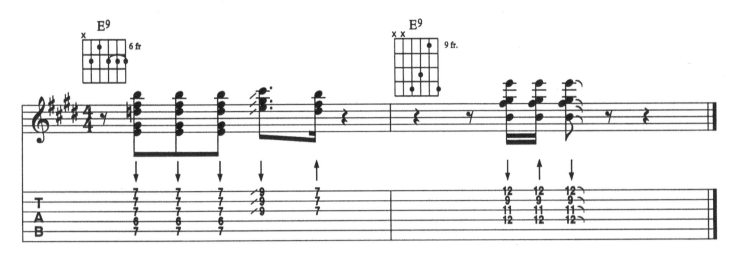

The slide in this pattern is used in a different way in *Slow Urban Blues Strum #2* (see the **BLUES** chapter). The high E9 chord at the end of the pattern could be any higher inversion of the original chord. The strum would also work if you played the same inversion throughout. Since it's a two-bar pattern, *Sliding Funk Pattern #3* works in one-chord vamp songs like Sly Stone's "Thank You" and "I Want to Take You Higher," and Wilson Pickett's "Don't Knock My Love" and "Engine Number 9."

Funk Ballad #1 🔷

Tempo: Slow to moderate funk

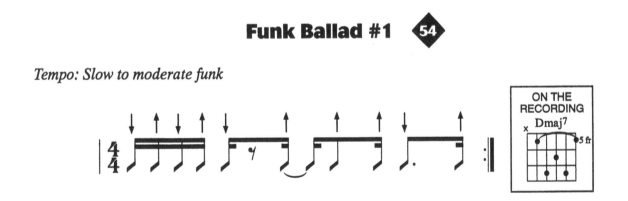

Sliding Funk Patterns #1 and *#2* are used often in soul ballads. This pattern is another ballad or moderately slow funk groove, first popularized in Marvin Gaye's "What's Goin' On" and "Let's Get It On" as well as the Jackson Five's "Never Can Say Goodbye."

Funk Ballad #2

Tempo: Slow to moderate funk

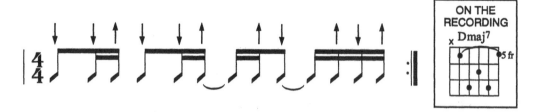

One of many possible variations of *Funk Ballad #1*, for tunes like "Feel Like Makin' Love" (Roberta Flack) and "Do Your Thing" (Isaac Hayes).

Funk Ballad #3 ◈55

Tempo: Slow to moderate funk

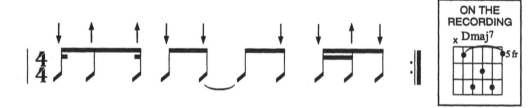

This is another variation, as in "Tonight Is Right" (Keith Washington).

Disco/Scratch Rhythm #1 ◈56

Tempo: Moderate funk

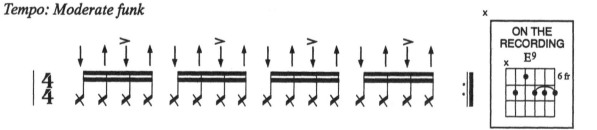

This non-stop sixteenth-note rhythm was popularized in early disco tunes like the Bee Gees' "Jive Talkin'." It is played with normal or muted chords. In tunes like "Shaft" (Isaac Hayes), a rhythmically rocking wah-wah pedal gave it a distinctive sound. It can be varied in countless ways, such as by removing a sixteenth-note strum or two, as in the two patterns that follow.

Disco/Scratch Rhythm #2

Tempo: Moderate funk

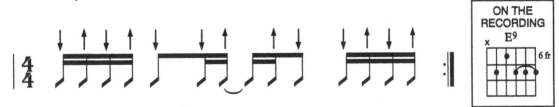

This is heard in "Night Fever" (Bee Gees), "Suicide Blonde" (INXS), and "I Will Survive" (Gloria Gaynor).

Disco/Scratch Rhythm #3 57

Tempo: Moderate funk

This is yet another variation.

Soul Shuffle #1 58

Tempo: Moderate to fast rock shuffle

Essentially the same as *Urban Blues Comping #1,* this strum works in tunes like "Don't Mess With Bill" (the Marvelettes), "Morning Train (Nine to Five)" (Sheena Easton), and "Heat Wave" and "Jimmy Mack" (Martha and the Vandellas).

Tempo: Moderate rock shuffle

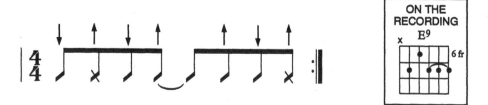

This has a slightly looser feel than *Soul Shuffle #1*, as in "How Sweet It Is (to Be Loved by You)" (Marvin Gaye, James Taylor) and "The Way You Do the Things You Do" (the Temptations).

Soul 6/8 Time #1 59

Tempo: Slow to moderate ballad

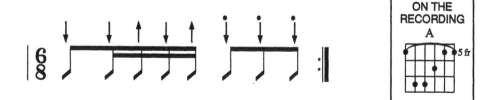

This has a very clipped, taut 6/8 feel, as in "Anyone Who Had A Heart" (Dionne Warwick), "I've Been Loving You Too Long (To Stop Now)" (Otis Redding), and "End Of the Road" (Boyz II Men).

Soul 6/8 Time #2 60

Tempo: Slow to moderate ballad

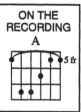

This is a variation of *#1*.

Tempo: Slow to moderate ballad

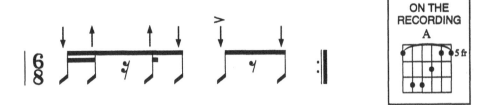

This is a very syncopated variation of 6/8 time.

Cross-References

R&B and rock have always shared musical ideas, and both forms derive from the blues. That's why rock and blues strums are useful in R&B/funk/soul music. All the boogie-woogie patterns occur, and many early soul hits use "Hi-Heel Sneakers" strums (e.g., Marvin Gaye's "Can I Get a Witness," also covered by the Rolling Stones).

BLUES Chapter: *Basic Boogie Lick, Basic Boogie Lick (Moveable), Boogie/Rock Lick #1, Boogie/Rock Lick (Moveable), Boogie/Rock Lick #2, Urban Blues Comping #1 to #4, Slow Urban Blues Strum (6/8), Slow Urban Blues Strum #2.*

ROCK Chapter: *Rock Boogie #1, #1 Variation, #2 and #3, Rock Boogie Shuffle #1 and #2, "Hi-Heel Sneakers" Boogie Rock/Strum #1 and #2, Latin Rock #1 to #5, 6/8 Rock Strum #1 and #2, 6/8 Rock Arpeggio #1 and #2.*

METAL, PUNK, AND GRUNGE

These terms mean different things to different people, but for guitarists they all have a common denominator: *distortion*. It can come from an over-driven tube amp, an effects processor, an over-drive channel in a solid-state amplifier, a foot pedal, or any combination of these*. Metal and punk are both rock, and they use the rock strumming and picking patterns. Distortion changes the way you play, and many strumming patterns have evolved that are peculiar to metal and punk.

Metal is driven by heavy guitar riffs. There are chord/rhythm riffs and single-note melody riffs. (A *riff* is a short musical phrase that is repeated over and over.) The chord/strumming riffs that follow are not lifted from specific tunes. They are an exploration of typical ways to construct metal riffs. Naturally, they are all to be played on electric guitar with the distortion turned up to "eleven."

* See **EQUIPMENT APPENDIX**

Power Chords

Power chords are the two-note and three-note chords popularized by Chuck Berry that go back to the early blues/boogie licks. They first appear in this book in the **BLUES** section, with the *Basic Boogie Licks*. Heavy metal rhythm guitarists play power chords more often than standard guitar chords, and they use these three shapes (the third note of each chord, in parenthesis, is optional):

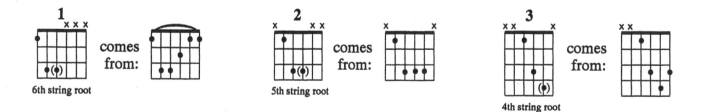

Power chords have no thirds, just a root and fifth, so they are written like this: A5, G5, C5, etc. Here are three ways to play A5:

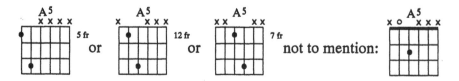

Metal Riff with Sustain #1

Tempo: Moderate to fast rock

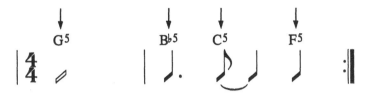

Distortion makes the electric guitar sustain. Many riffs contain long-sustaining power chords. This happens often during a verse; a busier (more chops) pattern is played for the chorus.

Metal Riff with Sustain #2 62

Tempo: Fast rock

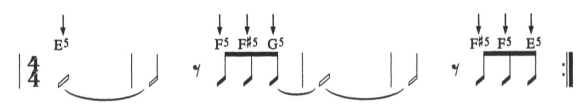

This pattern would have a lot of empty space if it weren't for pounding drums and a sustaining wall of rhythm guitar grunge.

Metal Riff with Sustain #3 62

Tempo: Moderate to fast rock

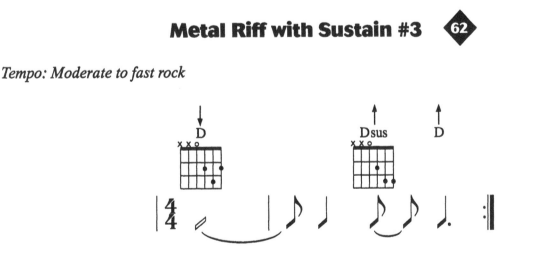

This is a third example of the infinite possible variations of sustain riffs.

Metal Rock Riff #1 ◆63◆

Tempo: Moderate to fast rock

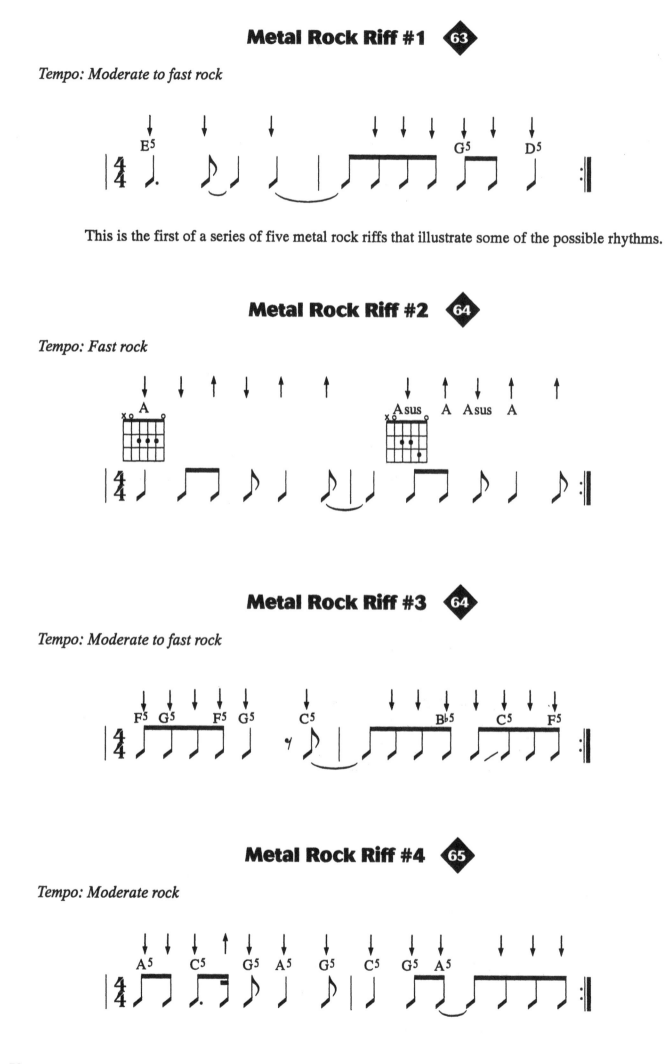

This is the first of a series of five metal rock riffs that illustrate some of the possible rhythms.

Metal Rock Riff #2 ◆64◆

Tempo: Fast rock

Metal Rock Riff #3 ◆64◆

Tempo: Moderate to fast rock

Metal Rock Riff #4 ◆65◆

Tempo: Moderate rock

Metal Rock Riff #5 ◆65◆

Tempo: Fast rock

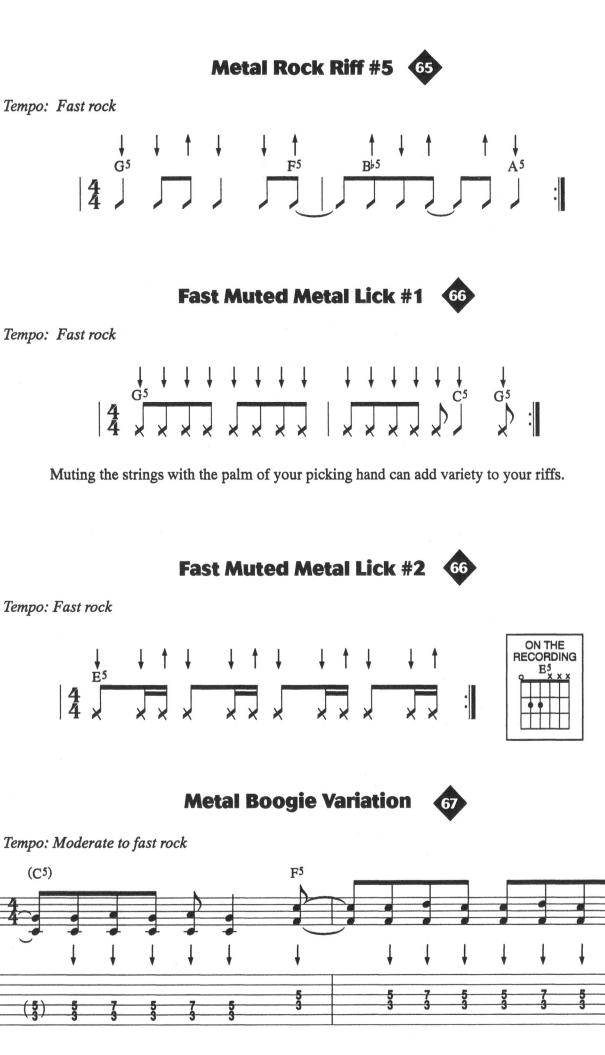

Fast Muted Metal Lick #1 ◆66◆

Tempo: Fast rock

Muting the strings with the palm of your picking hand can add variety to your riffs.

Fast Muted Metal Lick #2 ◆66◆

Tempo: Fast rock

ON THE
RECORDING
E⁵
x x x

Metal Boogie Variation ◆67◆

Tempo: Moderate to fast rock

There are countless ways to syncopate and vary the standard Chuck Berry-style bass/boogie lick. This is one.

Metal Open-String Riff 68

Tempo: Fast rock

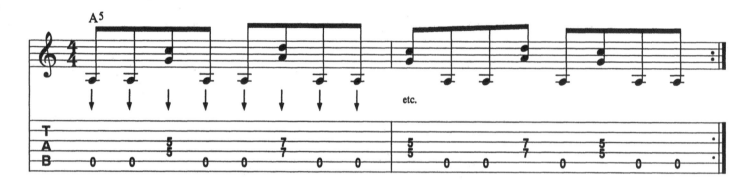

This is typical of the many riffs that take advantage of an open bass string. Similar licks could be played using the open E (6th) and D (4th) strings. It creates a powerful, droning, rhythmic riff.

Funk/Metal Riff #1 69

Tempo: Moderate funk/rock

Is there such a thing as funk/metal? Think of the grooves in tunes like "Way Cool Jr." (Ratt), "Walk This Way," and "Love In An Elevator" (Aerosmith), "I Love Rock 'n' Roll" (Joan Jett), "Kick 'n' Fight" (Britny Fox) . . . think of the Red Hot Chili Peppers!

Funk/Metal Riff #2 69

Tempo: Moderate funk/rock

This is another, simpler approach to funk/metal.

Punk Strum #1

Tempo: Fast rock

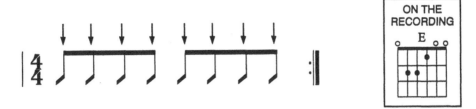

Punk tends to rely on simple, repetitious, loud strums to push the beat. The guitarist often uses first-position chords. This all-downstroke strum is about as basic as you can get.

Punk Strum #2 71

Tempo: Fast rock

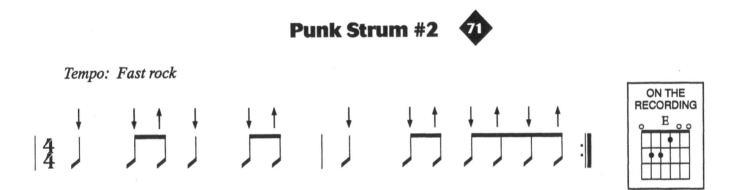

Play this one several times and you'll understand why they often call it "thrash" metal.

Punk Strum #3 71

Tempo: Moderate to fast rock

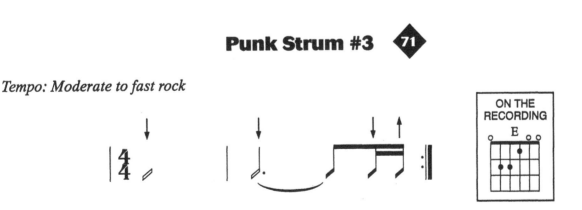

This is like the metal sustain riffs, only simpler.

Punk Strum #4   ◆72

Tempo: Moderate to fast rock

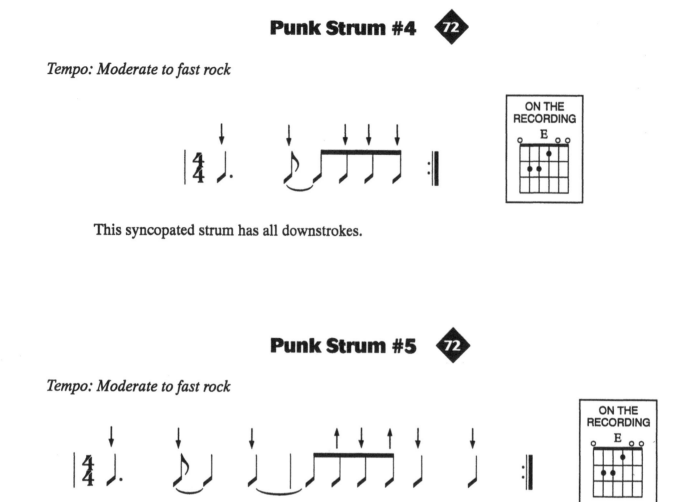

This syncopated strum has all downstrokes.

Punk Strum #5   ◆72

Tempo: Moderate to fast rock

This is a slightly more extended version of *Punk Strum #4*. It's similar to *Metal Rock Riff #1*, but simpler.

Cross-References

Metal grew out of rock, and it uses many rock strums for uptempo tunes and ballads. Blues patterns also occur in metal.

BLUES Chapter: *Rural Blues Shuffle #1* and *#2, Rural Blues Fingerpicking Pattern (Texas Style) #1* and *#2, Shuffle Blues Lick #1* to *#3,* and all the boogie licks: *Basic Boogie Lick, Basic Boogie Lick (Moveable), Boogie-Rock Lick #1, Boogie-Rock Lick (Moveable), Boogie-Rock Lick #2.*

ROCK Chapter: *Basic Rock #1* to *#3, Rock/Funk #1* to *#4, Rock Ballad #1* to *#4, Fingerpicking Rock Ballad #1* to *#4,* and all the boogie licks: *Rock Boogie #1, #1 Variation, Rock Boogie #2* and *3, Rock Boogie Shuffle #1* and *#2.*

Punk uses all of the boogie licks from the **ROCK** and **BLUES** chapters.

COUNTRY

Today's country music is a blend of traditional country, blues, rock, pop, and western swing. Since blues and rock guitar backup is covered in other chapters of this book, the patterns that follow are of the more traditional country variety. For example, the Carter strum was popular in 1930s string bands and 1940s bluegrass bands, and it's a staple in modern country. Early country fingerpicking was derived from rural blues, but Merle Travis and Chet Atkins put a new twist on fingerpicking, which is documented in this chapter.

Contemporary country music often borrows rhythms and guitar styles from 1960s and 1970s rock and blues. So look in the **ROCK** chapter for straight-eighths rock strums and boogie-woogie backup licks. There is always a back-to-the-roots/traditionalist element popping up in country music that makes use of the patterns in this chapter.

Bluegrass Strum #1 (The Carter Lick) 73

Tempo: Moderate to fast

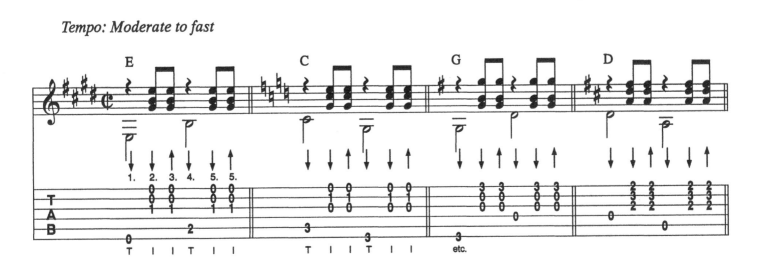

Most guitarists use a flatpick for this strum, but Maybelle Carter, who popularized it, did it finger style, as did Lester Flatt and other early bluegrass players:

1. Pick a bass note with your thumb. It should be the *keynote* (C in the key of C, E in the key of E).

2. Brush *down* on the treble strings with your thumb or the back of the index or middle finger.

3. Brush *up* on the treble strings with your index or middle finger.

4. Pick another bass note with your thumb, preferably the 5th in the chord (G in a C chord, B in an E chord).

5. Repeat steps 2 and 3 (brush down and up on the treble strings).

The alternating bass notes (root and 5th) are an important part of the strum. Country rhythm guitarists use it, as well as bluegrassers, in "Jambalaya" and "I Saw the Light" (Hank Williams), "Wabash Cannonball" and "Wildwood Flower" (the Carter Family), and "I Walk the Line" (Johnny Cash).

EQUIPMENT NOTE: Usually played on acoustic guitar.

Tempo: Fast cut-time

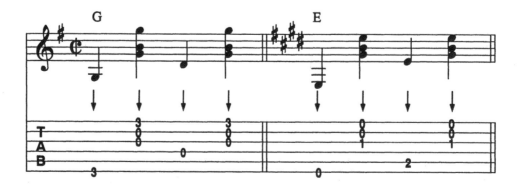

This is the same as the previous strum–streamlined for speed. The upstrokes are removed. The alternating bass remains. Some examples are "Orange Blossom Special," "Roll in My Sweet Baby's Arms," "Rocky Top," "Mountain Dew," "Foggy Mountain Breakdown," and the fast part of "Dueling Banjos."

EQUIPMENT NOTE: Usually played on acoustic guitar.

Bluegrass Strum #3

Tempo: Moderate to slow country shuffle

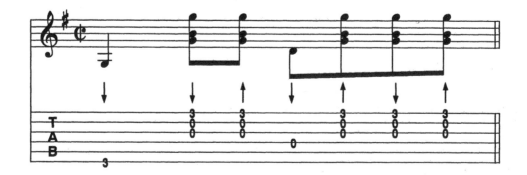

This is like *Bluegrass Strum #1*, with an extra upstroke added to fill out the rhythm in a slower tempo, as in "Your Cheatin' Heart" (Hank Williams), "Will the Circle Be Unbroken" (Carter Family and many others), "Blue Eyes Crying in the Rain" (Willie Nelson), and "Cool Water" (Sons of the Pioneers).

EQUIPMENT NOTE : Usually played on acoustic guitar.

Country Strum #1

Tempo: Moderate to bright country shuffle

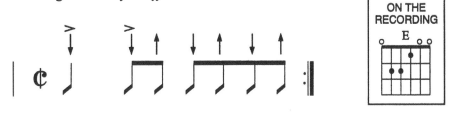

The first downstroke can be aimed at the bass strings, as in the bluegrass strums (but less precisely). Some examples are "Act Naturally" (Buck Owens, the Beatles), "Take Me Home, Country Roads" (John Denver), "Mama Tried" (Merle Haggard), "Wake Up Little Susie" (the Everly Brothers), and "Back in the Saddle Again" (Gene Autrey).

Country Strum #2

Tempo: Moderate to slow country shuffle

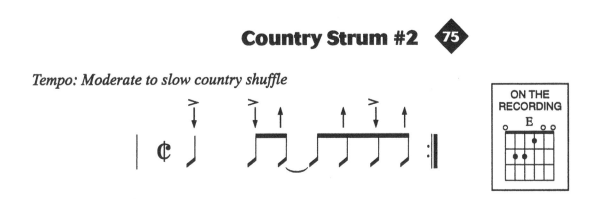

Play slower and more syncopated than *Country Strum #1*, as in "Bye Bye Love" (the Everly Brothers), "I Can't Help It If I'm Still in Love With You" (Hank Williams, Linda Ronstadt), "Detroit City" (Bobby Bare), and "Don't Rock the Jukebox" (Alan Jackson).

Honky Tonk Strum

Tempo: Moderately slow to moderately bright shuffle

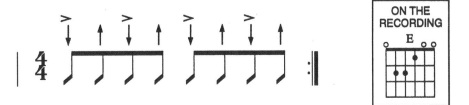

This has a stronger shuffle beat than *Country Strum #1* or *#2*. It is often accompanied by a walking bass and is used in rowdy honky tonk tunes like "I Never Knew God Made Honky Tonk Angels" (Hank Thompson), "Honky Tonk Blues" and "Move It on Over" (Hank Williams, Sr. and Hank Williams, Jr.), and "Honky Tonk Man" (Johnny Horton, Dwight Yoakam).

Bluegrass Waltz

Tempo: Slow to fast waltz

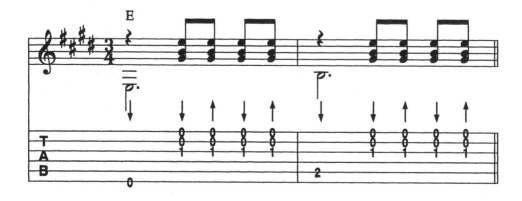

As in the other bluegrass strums, you alternate the root and 5th bass notes. Try this on "I'm So Lonesome I Could Cry" (Hank Williams), "Are You Lonesome Tonight" (Elvis Presley), and classic waltzes like "Amazing Grace," "Goodnight, Irene," and "Tennessee Waltz."

Country Waltz 78

Tempo: Slow to fast waltz

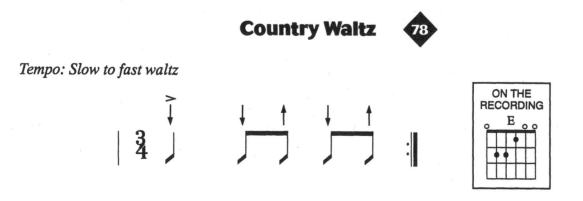

This is the same as the *Bluegrass Waltz*, but you strum instead of picking an individual bass note. The two waltzes are interchangeable; the *Bluegrass Waltz* has more of an old-fashioned country sound. Try the *Country Waltz* on "Norwegian Wood" (the Beatles), "You Light up My Life" (Debby Boone), "Lucille" (Kenny Rogers),and "Mamas Don't Let Your Babies Grow up to Be Cowboys" (Willie Nelson and Waylon Jennings).

EQUIPMENT NOTE: Use acoustic guitar, or electric guitar enhanced by flanger, phase shifter, etc. (see the **EQUIPMENT APPENDIX**).

Travis-Style Fingerpicking Pattern #1 79

Tempo: Moderate to fast shuffle

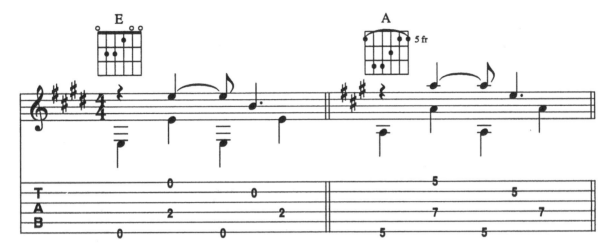

All Travis-style picking is based on a steady, on-every-downbeat, alternating thumb/bass pattern. The index and middle fingers play the higher strings on or off the beat, picking melody or rhythmic fills. The thumb/bass pattern never wavers. For a more authentic Travis, or Chet Atkins, sound, damp the bass notes with the palm of your right hand.

The key-of-A pattern above, is the same as the preceding key-of-E pattern, turned into a moveable lick. It's based on the barred E chord. Both *Travis-Style Fingerpicking Patterns* are also rockabilly patterns. They work well in songs like "Blue Suede Shoes" (Carl Perkins, Elvis Presley), "That's All Right, Mama" and "Good Rockin' Tonight" (Elvis Presley), "Crazy Little Thing Called Love" (Queen), and "All My Loving" (the Beatles), as well as country hits like "My Baby Thinks He's a Train" (Roseanne Cash) and "Heartbroke" (Ricky Skaggs).

EQUIPMENT NOTE: The *Travis-Style Fingerpicking Patterns* sound good on acoustic or electric guitar, but use an electric to get the Travis sound. For a rockabilly sound, play an electric guitar with "slap-echo": digital or analog delay (see **EQUIPMENT APPENDIX**) will recreate that Sun Records sound.

Travis-Style Fingerpicking Pattern #2 79

Tempo: Moderate to fast shuffle

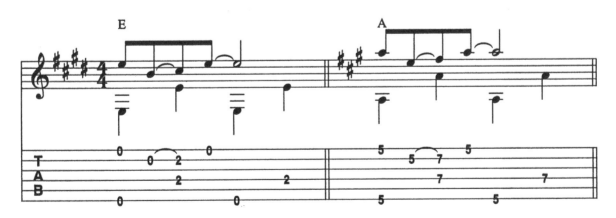

This is a variation of *Travis-Style Fingerpicking Pattern #1*. Use it as a repeated pattern or combine it with #1 and make a two-bar phrase.

EQUIPMENT NOTE: Same as *Travis-Style Fingerpicking Pattern #1*.

Banjo Roll #1 ◆80◆

Tempo: Fast cut-time

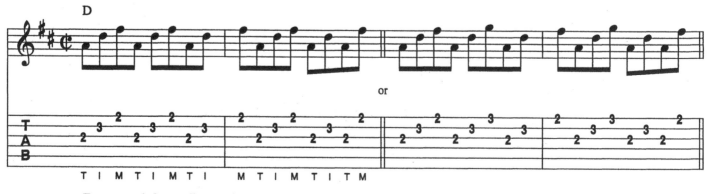

Borrowed from five-string banjo picking, this pattern is a tasteful backup lick in songs like "Mama Tried" (Merle Haggard) and "Guitar Man" (Elvis Presley). The second sample has the same picking as the first, with some left-hand movement added.

Banjo Roll #2 ◆80◆

Tempo: Fast two-beat

This is a variation of *Banjo Roll #1*.

Cajun Strum ◆81◆

Tempo: Moderate to fast rock

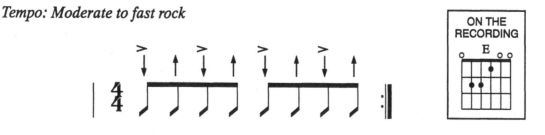

On paper this looks like the *Honky Tonk Strum*, but the *Cajun Strum* has more of a straight-eighths rock feel, rather than a shuffle beat, as in "Down at the Twist and Shout" (Mary-Chapin Carpenter) and "Louisiana Man" (Doug Kershaw).

The "straight-eighths rock feel" has eight beats to the bar and lacks the "dotted note" or "triplet" feel of a shuffle beat. To feel the difference between a straight-eighths and shuffle rhythm, listen to the recording and compare the *Cajun Strum* to the *Honky Tonk Strum*.

Cross-References

A strumming acoustic guitar has always been the backbone of the country sound. It still is, but today's acoustic guitarist may be strumming a rock groove or a boogie-woogie feel.

ROCK Chapter: *Basic Rock #1 to #3, Rock Shuffle #1 and #2, Rock Boogie #1 to #3, Rock Boogie Variation, Rock Boogie Shuffle #1 and #2, "Hi-Heel Sneakers" Boogie/Rock Strum #1 to #4, Rock Ballad #1 to #4.*

Country with a Southern-rock flavor may feature an electric guitar playing blues boogie licks. The western swing feel is often evoked by playing blues comping strums.

BLUES Chapter: *Rural Blues Shuffle #1 and #2, Fingerpicking Boogie Lick #1 and #2, Basic Boogie Lick, Basic Boogie Lick (Moveable, Boogie/Rock Lick #1, Boogie/Rock Lick (Moveable) and #2, Urban Blues Comping #1 to #4.*

Acoustic country guitarists often borrow fingerpicking patterns from blues and rock for ballads and moderate-tempo tunes.

BLUES Chapter: *Rural Blues Fingerpicking Pattern (Rag Style) #1 and #2.*

ROCK Chapter: *Fingerpicking Rock #2 and #4, Fingerpicking Rock Ballad #1 to #4.*

Some contemporary country songs have a rhythm groove reminiscent of 1960s and 1970s R&B.

R&B/FUNK/SOUL Chapter:*Basic Sparse Soul/Rock Strums #1 to #4, Basic Soul/Rock Strums #1 to #4, Funk Ballad #1 to #3.*

Country songs regularly evoke the vintage rockabilly sound by playing fingerpicking and boogie patterns from the **ROCK** and **BLUES** chapters.

ROCK Chapter: *Rockabilly Fingerpicking #1 to #5, all "Boogie" Strums.*

BLUES Chapter: all *"Boogie" Strums.*

FOLK MUSIC

To some people, "folk music" means British, Irish, American, or any nation's songs that are so old their composer is unknown, e.g., "Skip to My Lou," "Careless Love," and "Greensleeves." To others, it means early acoustic blues or string band (country) music. For many people it refers to the folk/pop revival of the late 1950s, early 1960s led by city musicians like the Kingston Trio, the Weavers, and the Limelighters. Singer/songwriters of the 1980s and 1990s who drew upon musical styles of the sixties folksters were called "new wave folk." The bottom line is: It's folk if it highlights acoustic guitar and other unelectrified instruments and is less slick and commercial than most pop music.

Most of the picking and strumming styles needed to perform "folk" music are found in the **ROCK, BLUES,** and **COUNTRY** chapters. What follows are some patterns not found elsewhere that are heard on recordings of Joan Baez, Tracy Chapman, Gordon Lightfoot, Suzanne Vega, and other pop artists who emphasize acoustic guitar in their performing and recording.

Folk Ballad Arpeggio #1 ◆82◆

Tempo: Slow to moderate, straight-eighths beat (like a rock ballad)

Though it can be played with a flatpick, this arpeggio pattern is often played with the thumb and three fingers. It has a gentle, soothing feel that suits songs like "Suzanne" (Leonard Cohen, Judy Collins), "The First Time Ever I Saw Your Face" (Ewan MacColl, Robert Flack), and "All My Trials" (Joan Baez and others).

Folk Ballad Arpeggio #2

Tempo: Slow to moderate, straight-eighths beat

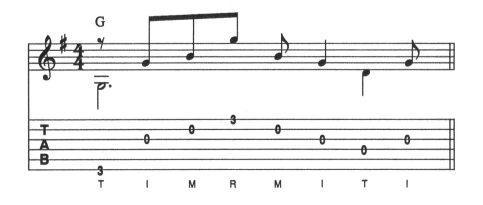

This is a variation of #1, as in "Danny Boy" (recorded by countless artists) and "Leaving on a Jet Plane" (Peter, Paul and Mary).

Folk Ballad Arpeggio #3

Tempo: Slow to moderate, straight-eighths beat

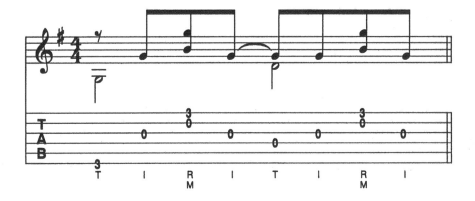

This has a slightly stronger beat than #1 or #2, as in "Both Sides Now" (Joni Mitchell, Judy Collins), and "Dona Dona" (Joan Baez, Donovan). It can also be played as a slow shuffle beat, as in "Hush, Little Baby," the lullaby that was turned into a rock song ("Mockingbird") or "Tumbling Tumbleweeds" (the Sons of the Pioneers).

Tempo: Moderate waltz

This is another thumb-and-three-fingers pattern, as in "Goodnight, Irene" (Leadbelly, the Weavers) and "Satisfied Mind" (Ian and Sylvia, Bob Dylan).

Folk Waltz Arpeggio #2 85

Tempo: Moderate waltz

This has a lighter, airier feel than *Folk Waltz #1*, as in "Scarborough Fair" (adapted by Simon and Garfunkel), and "Plaisir d'Amour" (Joan Baez).

Folk Fingerpicking #1

Tempo: Moderate to fast cut-time

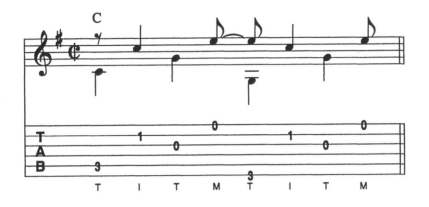

Derived from the raggy blues styles (see **BLUES** chapter), this works for tunes like "It Ain't Me, Babe" (Bob Dylan, Johnny Cash), "Don't Think Twice, It's All Right" (Dylan; Peter, Paul and Mary), and "The Boxer" (Simon and Garfunkel).

Folk Fingerpicking #2

Tempo: Moderate cut-time

There are countless variations of *Folk Fingerpicking #1*, and this is a popular one, as in "The Last Thing on My Mind" (Tom Paxton, Joan Baez, Doc Watson, and many others), "Blowin' in the Wind" (Dylan; Peter, Paul and Mary), and "Puff the Magic Dragon" (Peter, Paul and Mary).

Calypso Fingerpicking

Tempo: Moderate to bright

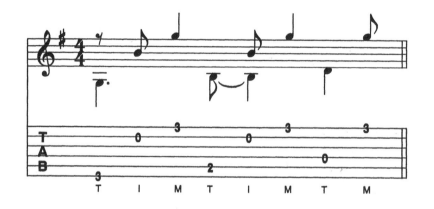

Calypso was a mainstay of the folk boom of the late 1950s; that's why the Kingston Trio was so named. This fingerpicking pattern works for folk hits like "Sloop John B." (the Kingston Trio, the Beach Boys) and "Lemon Tree" (Peter, Paul and Mary).

Calypso Strum #1 88

Tempo: Moderate to bright

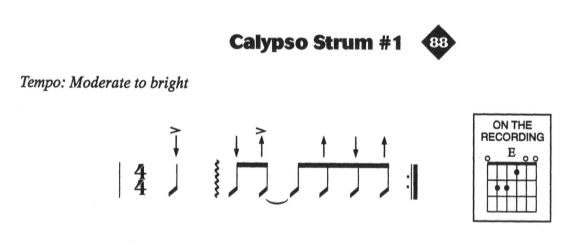

This is a strumming version of the *Calypso Fingerpicking* pattern, as in "Jamaica Farewell" (Harry Belafonte and many others), "Banana Boat (Day-O)" (Belafonte), and the tunes mentioned for *Calypso Fingerpicking*. You can do this strum with a flatpick, but many folkies used their hand like this:

- Brush down on the top (treble) three or four strings with the fingernails, using a loose strum that includes three or four fingers.

- Brush up with the thumb, hitting the strings with the thumbnail.

The "rasgueado" effect, indicated by the wiggly line (⅜), is done by unwinding the fingers of your strumming hand from the pinkie to the index finger as you strum. This creates a rippling strum. It's a popular Spanish guitar technique.

Calypso Strum #2

Tempo: Bright

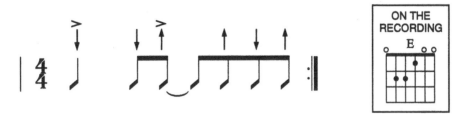

This is a faster version of *Calypso Strum #1*, as in "Marianne" (the Easy Riders, Belafonte, and others) and "Tijuana Jail" (Kingston Trio).

Basic Plucking Pattern

Tempo: Slow to fast cut-time

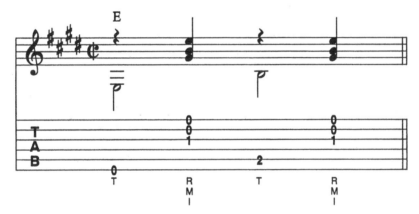

This very simple pattern is often taught to beginners as a first strum. The index, middle, and ring fingers simultaneously pluck upward on the top three strings, and the thumb alternates bass notes. It brings to mind Burl Ives' folk hits like "Skip to My Lou," "The Fox," and "Froggie Went A-Courtin'."

Plucking Pattern #2

Tempo: Moderate cut-time

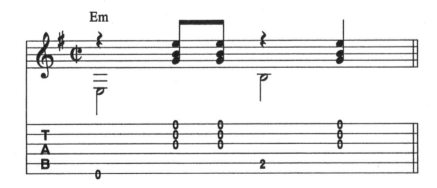

This variation of the *Basic Plucking Pattern* is often used on Russian songs ("Moscow Nights"), Jewish folk songs ("O Hanukah"), Christmas songs ("Twelve Days of Christmas"), and children's songs ("I've Been Working on the Railroad").

Waltz/Plucking Pattern

Tempo: Slow to moderate waltz

This pattern fits the same categories of songs as *Plucking Patterns #1* and *#2:* three-quarter-time tunes such as "Cockles and Mussels," "Tumbalalaika," "Cielito Lindo," "What Child Is This?" and "On Top of Old Smokey."

March/Plucking Pattern 92

Tempo: Moderate to fast march

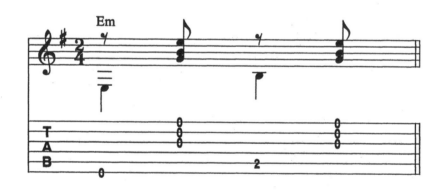

This pattern is used for march-tempo folk tunes like "Johnny, I Hardly Knew Ye," "I Know an Old Lady," and "Oats, Peas, Beans and Barley."

Cross-References

Folk music borrows strums and fingerpicking patterns from the blues, rock, and country bags. The following list includes most of the patterns from those three chapters.

COUNTRY Chapter: *Bluegrass Strum #1 to #3, Country Strum #1 and #2, Honky Tonk Strum, Bluegrass Waltz, Country Waltz, Travis-Style Fingerpicking Pattern #1 and #2, Cajun Strum.*

ROCK Chapter: *Basic Rock #1 to #3, Rock Shuffle #1 and #2, Fast Rock Shuffle, Fast Rock Strum, Rock/Funk #1 to #4, Fingerpicking Rock #1 to #4, Rock Ballad #1 to #4, Fingerpicking Rock Ballad #1 to #4,* and all the *Boogie licks: Rock Boogie #1 to #3, Rock Boogie Variation, Rock Boogie Shuffle #1 and #2.*

BLUES Chapter: *Rural Blues Shuffle, Strum #1 and #2, Rural Blues Fingerpicking Pattern (Rag Style) #1 and #2 and (Texas Style) #1 and #2, Basic Boogie Lick, Basic Boogie Lick (Moveable), Boogie/Rock Lick #1, Boogie Rock Lick (Moveable), Boogie/Rock Lick #2*

EQUIPMENT APPENDIX

Here is a description of musical equipment that was mentioned in this book. The *electronic effects* (reverb, echo, delay, chorus, flanger, phase shifter, distortion, and tremolo) can have several shapes. They can be built into an amplifier, an effects processor, a footpedal, or an individual rack-mounted unit.

Chorus: an electronic effect that "doubles" an electric guitar's notes, making a six-string guitar sound like a twelve string. It enriches and fattens a guitar's tone. It's often used for fingerpicking, background arpeggios, and solos.

Delay (Analog and Digital): an electronic effect that produces many types of echo.

Distortion: the fuzzy, screaming guitar sound associated with loud rock and metal. It can be produced by electronic effects or by turning up an amplifier (especially a tube amp) so loud that the speakers "break up" or distort the sound.

Echo: the repeating, reverberating, enriched sound you get singing or playing in a room that bounces sound around, such as a shower, gymnasium, or an echo chamber. "Delay" and "reverb" are electronic effects that produce echo.

Flanger: an electronic effect that produces a rhythmic sweep effect of variable intensity and speed. It's similar to a phase shifter.

Overdrive: the fuzzy, distorted sound an amp produces when it is turned up so loud that the sound "breaks up." A variable overdrive channel is often built into amplifiers. It allows you to get a range of distortion (from slightly fuzzy to completely broken up) at any volume. Electronic effects that produce the same sounds are called "overdrive."

Phase Shifter: an electronic effect that adds a sweeping, wave-like sound of variable depth and speed to your guitar's tone. It was originally invented to imitate the oscillating effect produced by a Hammond organ's Leslie speaker.

Reverb: an electronic effect that creates echo, often built into amplifiers.

Slapback Echo: the particular type of echo associated with rockabilly music and the Sun Records' sound. It's characterized by a brief but powerful single repeated signal; it can be produced by delay effects.

Solid State Amp: an amplifier that has transistors instead of tubes.

Tremolo: an electronic device that was built into many early tube amps. It produces an oscillating, wavering sound. It was pioneered by Bo Diddley and heard often in surf music and early rock, especially on ballads.

Tube Amp: an electric guitar amplifier powered by tubes instead of transistors. Early amps were all tube amps. They distorted more easily and had a warmer sound than solid state amps, and many manufacturers are producing them again, often with a retro, vintage appearance.

GUITAR STRINGS

Strings come in different gauges (thicknesses). Fatter strings have a richer, fuller sound, but they are harder on your fretting hand than thinner strings, and they are harder to bend or choke. So, the type of music you play determines which gauge of strings you use.

- Use heavy or medium gauge strings for strumming and fingerpicking, unless you bend a lot of strings when fingerpicking.

- Use light or super-light gauge strings if you do a lot of string-bending. Some players use medium gauge strings except for the top two or three (treble) strings. They use lighter gauges on these because that's where most string-bending occurs.